MEN *and* DEPRESSION

About the Authors

Theresa Francis-Cheung (BA King's College, Cambridge;
MA King's College, London) is a freelance health writer.
Her books include: *Androgen Disorders in Women: The
Most Neglected Hormone Problem* (Hunter House, 1999),
Pregnancy Weight Management (Adams Media, 2000),
*Cope with the Biological Clock: How to Make the Right
Decisions about Motherhood* (Hodder and Stoughton, 2001),
A Woman's Guide to Healthy Living through Her 30s
(Adams Media, 2001), *Manage Your Weight and Fitness
through Childbirth* (Hodder and Stoughton, 2001), and
Worry: The Root of All Evil (Gill and Macmillan, 2002)

A health consultant and teacher before writing full-time,
Theresa lives in Windsor with husband Ray and their two
young children, Robert and Ruth.

Robin Grey is a British Association of Counselling
Registered Practitioner. His special areas of concern are
mental health and learning difficulties. He has worked as a
counsellor for MIND and various central London health
authorities. He also tutors counselling skills and has his
own private practice.

Robin lives with his partner in South London.

MEN *and*
DEPRESSION

Helping him, helping you

Thorsons

Thorsons
An Imprint of HarperCollins*Publishers*
77–85 Fulham Palace Road,
Hammersmith, London W6 8JB

The Thorsons website address is: www.thorsons.com

and *Thorsons*

are trademarks of
HarperCollins*Publishers* Limited

Published by Thorsons 2002

10 9 8 7 6 5 4 3 2 1

© Theresa Francis-Cheung and Robin Grey 2002

Theresa Francis-Cheung and Robin Grey assert the moral right to be identified as the authors of this work

A catalogue record for this book is available from the British Library

ISBN 0 00 711297 1

Printed and bound in Great Britain by
Creative Print and Design Wales, Ebbw Vale

This book is dedicated to the memory of
Menko Ennen (1895–1918)

Acknowledgements

Thanks to all the people who spoke to me about the impact on their lives of depression in a male partner, family member, colleague or friend. Case histories have been modified and names have been changed to protect identities, but I am truly grateful for their openness, honesty and willingness to discuss a painful and difficult subject.

Thanks also to all the experts, doctors, mental health nurses, psychiatrists, psychologists, psychotherapists, counsellors, teachers and social workers I encountered in my research, who willingly gave me their time.

Thank you to Robin Grey. His knowledge, guidance and male perspective gave the book its substance. His feedback, insight, editing and help made the book possible.

A big thank you to my agent, Michael Alcock, for his advice, encouragement and charm. Thank you also to Cathy Fischgrund.

Thank you to my editor, Wanda Whiteley, for commissioning me to write about such a challenging subject. Her guidance and advice during the creation of the book were invaluable. Thanks also to all the staff at Thorsons.

Thank you to Dr Priscilla Stuckey for her invaluable insight and developmental editing.

Thanks to my brother Terry and to the support of family and friends. And finally, special gratitude to my husband Ray and our two children Robert and Ruth, for their patience, support, enthusiasm and love while I went into exile to complete this project.

Contents

A Word from Robin Grey

Depression impacts men at different ages and life stages, regardless of age, race, sexual preference or social or economic background. It may be a reaction to one or more life events, or it may simply be a feeling that 'something isn't quite right'. Yet such is the stigma attached to depression in men, it is unlikely that a depressed man will want to seek help and support. It is easier for him to hope that it will get better in time, or to try and ignore his feelings, pushing them to the back of his mind in the hope that they will go away if he just keeps busy or puts up a front for others.

It can be extremely difficult to be the partner, relative or close friend of a man who is depressed. If he is your partner, the warmth and physical intimacy that you usually enjoy may be lacking. If he is your son, you may be worried but not know how much to interfere or when to give advice. He seems to have lost his zest for life, but you don't know how to talk to him about it. You want to help, but you don't know how. If he is your partner, you want to be with him, but you also want to break from the despondent mood which envelopes you both when you are together.

A common experience for those in a caring role is to want to do the very best for the man they care for so that things can get back to how they were. You may feel guilty that you are not doing enough to help him, or angry that he is not, in your view, doing enough to help himself. If you think you have tried all the avenues available to you and him, you may not know what else you can do. It is understandable to want to find a solution for him. It may seem clear to you what that solution is. But the more you try and solve his problem, the more you are investing in, hoping for and expecting a positive outcome. One of the hardest challenges for you is accepting that you alone cannot change the situation for him. If he rejects your help, or seems unwilling to help himself, this can leave you feeling rejected, hurt, angry, frustrated and helpless.

Whether you are reading this book as a partner, relative or friend of a depressed man, it is important to remember that there is help available and that you can access that help for him and for yourself. By picking up this book, you are taking the first step towards helping yourself cope with the situation, and helping him find a solution and some meaning from the experience.

Introduction

There remains a great deal of shame and guilt associated with depression in men, which often keeps people from acknowledging that a man can feel unhappy. If you are in a relationship with a depressed man, this puts you in a painful dilemma. You can either confront the man who is suffering and risk embarrassing him further, or you can conspire with him by ignoring or minimizing how he feels, a course that offers no hope of relief.

This book is intended for those who want to know what to do when a man they care about is depressed. His mood disorder could be mild or it could be severe. You may be a partner, a parent, a daughter, a son, a sibling, a colleague, a teacher or a friend. You may be the only person concerned, or you may be sharing the concern with other people or with professionals. Whatever the case, this book will help you to understand and cope. Case histories, information, advice and reassurance will show you that there is a way out of the dilemma. There are ways to help a man who is hurting, without humiliating him.

Part 1 will explore male depression – how it manifests, how you can recognize it, what puts a man at special risk, and how his depression may affect you. Part 2 offers practical advice on how to help him. You will also learn how to take care of your own physical and emotional health during the crisis.

Men who have known bouts of despair speak of it as a kind of living death, a deep darkness of the soul, where the self wages a struggle against loss, hopelessness and futility. Yet as intensely personal as the experience may seem, its effects spread beyond the individual into the circle of family, friends and work relationships. As the joy in life dissipates, an unhappy man pushes away companionship and intimacy, often leaving the people in his life to feel as alone, cold and helpless as he does. If you are in a relationship with a depressed man, the advice in this book will help you cope with your own feelings of shock, guilt, anger and despair.

Men, in general, seem less well equipped than women to handle the emotional and physical crisis of mood disorders, and are far less likely to talk about their problems with ease and openness. This book will help you encourage a man who seems to have lost his zest for life to help himself, and, if necessary, seek the help and support he needs to get through this difficult time.

Understanding Male Depression

It is the feeling that nothing is worthwhile that makes men ill and unhappy.

Dr Harold W Dodds

1

When a Man You Care About Is Depressed

Every day, in every way, things are getting worse and worse.

William F Buckley, Jr

When a man you care about is depressed, expect to experience a wide range of conflicting emotions:

You feel bewildered and afraid. You don't understand what is happening.

You are not sure how to cope. You are in shock.

You feel sad and shut out. You can't find a way to connect with him. You long for the man who was.

You feel frustrated and drained.

A part of you wants to walk away.

A part of you wants to pretend this isn't happening.

You feel guilty and anxious. Is it somehow your fault? Are you doing enough to help him?

You feel angry and resentful. Why can't he just pull himself together?

You may feel sad and hopeless about life yourself. Depression is like a black hole. It can draw you into an abyss of despair, blackness and turmoil.

Perhaps the most distressing feeling of all is one of powerlessness. You want to help, but you don't know how. Frequently the struggle to help is intense and deeply felt.

In my late twenties my boyfriend of the time became depressed. We had known each other for a year when he lost his job. He gradually became more reclusive. Eventually he would barely set foot outside his flat. Weeks of this aloneness would pass by.

I remember trying to help. I'd tidy the flat. Stock the fridge with his favourite foods. Talk about my day with enthusiasm. Look for job opportunities for him. Even pay some bills when he fell behind. I'd be lighthearted and pretend I didn't notice he was feeling down.

Other times I tried to get him to talk. Most of the time there was no response, but on occasion there would be outbursts of violence. He would scream out his hurt. He made me feel that I was the cause of his problems. At first I was relieved to have broken the silence, but then I was terrified of what he might do. He lashed out once. He often talked of suicide.

I expended lots of energy trying to find ways to help. With each failure I grew more and disappointed, frustrated and despondent. Gradually we drifted apart. I felt an overwhelming sense of alienation, sadness and failure.

Looking back, I can see that I tried too hard to fix the problem. I didn't pace myself. I didn't understand what I was dealing with. I lacked resources, information and advice. I started to feel depressed myself. I didn't know it at the time, but there were ways I could have helped. What I needed, but didn't seek out, was proper guidance and advice.

Research has shown that depression has a toxic effect on relationships, and people close to depressed men are more vulnerable to various disorders themselves. Fortunately, there is much you can do together with a depressed man to speed his recovery and to safeguard your relationship against the weight of the depression. There are also ways you can take care of your own emotional and physical health.

Bear in mind, though, that depression does not heal overnight. It takes time. In some cases it never really goes away, but there are ways to keep the situation under control. You will need a lot of *patience*. You will need a lot of *flexibility*. In your search for the most effective treatment, you may find that you need to keep adapting and changing your approach.

You also need to understand that there is only so much you can do. Often the depressed man seems incapable of seeking help for himself, but encouraging him to seek help is essential. If you start solving all his problems, you may make the situation worse.

Part of the recovery process will be his active participation in finding a solution.

Part of the helping process is recognizing that there is a limit to the amount you can do to help.

Having said this, there are things you can do and say, attitudes and boundaries you can establish, which are more helpful and useful than others when a man is depressed. His depression may or may not lose its intensity, but knowing you have done the best and most helpful thing can be comforting.

Understanding Depression

Before we explore what to do and how to help, it is important to educate yourself about this complex illness. Unfortunately, recognizing and acknowledging that a man you care about is depressed won't always be that easy. Depression in men is a subject shrouded in ignorance, misunderstanding and neglect.

....

I would wake up in the middle of the night with a violent churning sensation in my stomach. Waves of anxiety and sheer panic never left me. I cried silently. I felt guilty. I was plagued by gruesome and horrific

*images. I was terrified that I might be going crazy. I was far too
agitated to even think about organizing a doctor's appointment.
I didn't want to take drugs because I was worried about the
side-effects. I didn't trust or believe in therapy.*

Peter, age 40

When properly treated, up to 90 per cent of those suffering
from depression will see their symptoms alleviated. Depression
responds to treatment. The problem is that sufferers are not
coming forward for treatment.

A Canadian team of epidemiologists recently revealed that,
according to a mass telephone survey in the UK, around 87 per
cent of men and women suffering from depression are not seen,
or diagnosed as such, by their doctor. Only about 4 per cent of
depressives actually see the supposedly ideal expert specializing
in mental illness.

The great majority of those not seeking treatment and advice
for depression are men. The results of this concealment and
neglect have far-reaching implications.

According to the World Health Organization (WHO), one in
five people suffer from a bout of depression at some time in
their lives. Depression is remarkably common. In fact, it has
often been called 'the common cold of mental health problems'.
More than 5 per cent of Americans – some 15 million people –
suffer from clinical depression. Another 5 per cent experience
mild symptoms of being 'down in the dumps'.

In the next two decades, depression is set to become second
only to heart disease in the league of disabling diseases. It was
fourth 10 years ago. In the 2000 annual meeting of the World
Economic Forum in Switzerland, mental health experts from
around the globe urged governments and business to spend
more money on combating depression, which they described as
'the cancer of the 21st century'. Dr J Raymond DePaulo Jr, professor of psychiatry at Johns Hopkins University in Baltimore,

told the meeting that entire countries faced huge and increasing losses in productivity caused by depression.

The reluctance of sufferers to take their symptoms to a doctor, and the failure of many doctors actually to recognize the symptoms indicate a fast-approaching mental health crisis. At the heart of this crisis is ignorance: ignorance about what depression is, what causes it, how to recognize common symptoms, and what to do when it strikes.

Nowhere is this ignorance greater than when depression strikes a man.

Until recently, few people have focused entirely on depression in men. Fewer still have focused on the best ways to help. As a result, misunderstandings abound. These misunderstandings not only make it hard for a depressed man to ask for help, but they also make it hard for those around him to recognize the condition and know how to help.

Let's review some of the most common misunderstandings and myths.

1 Depression Is a 'Woman's Illness'

While depression is often traditionally thought of as an illness that mainly affects women, there is growing evidence to suggest that men are equally vulnerable, and actually more likely to take their own lives as a result.

Here are some facts:

- Male suicides outnumber female suicides by 4 to 1 in North America, Europe and Australia.
- The new millennium is witnessing an epidemic of suicides among young men. Suicide is the second most common cause, after accidents, of death in young men.
- 25 per cent of all suicides occur in men over the age of 65. For every six elderly women who kill themselves each year, 40 elderly men will attempt suicide.

- Over half the phone calls received by the Samaritans, the UK's major crisis helpline, are now from men, which is 30 per cent more than 10 years ago.

Far more men suffer from depression than is commonly realized. The problem is that men, and the people who care about them, are not familiar with recognizing depressive or anxious feelings, nor with seeking help, so men come to the attention of health professionals less often than women.

2 Men Don't Cry

Traditional gender stereotypes require women to express themselves emotionally and cultivate relationships. Men, by contrast, are encouraged to cultivate their public, assertive selves, often at the cost of their emotional expressiveness. In short, women are allowed to cry and talk about their problems. Men are not supposed to show or talk about their pain.

Depression carries with it the label of 'being emotional', seen as a feminine trait. Men may be too proud or emotionally stunted to acknowledge that their feelings are out of control. So what does a man do when he feels weak or vulnerable?

In his study of male depression, Terrence Real shows how many men feeling the shame of depression's 'unmanliness' are more likely to conceal their condition – not only from their friends and families, but from themselves.

A man may recognize that he 'isn't himself', but it wouldn't occur to him that he is depressed, or if it did he would dismiss the notion quickly. Acknowledging depression would be akin to saying he is weak or crazy or both. There is often a desperate search for other explanations. For instance, symptoms like being fully awake in the early hours of the morning, or a constant grinding in the stomach, may be explained away as insomnia or an upset stomach respectively.

Terrified of revealing that he may be in need of help, a man may hide his pain in behaviour we don't necessarily associate with depression. He may not cry or appear depressed, but he will cry out in other ways.

3 He Doesn't 'Seem' Depressed

A man tends to manifest symptoms of depression differently than a woman. His attempts to expel depression often fuel many of the problems we think of as typically male. He may not shed tears or blame himself as women tend to, but he is more likely to lash out with violent or abusive behaviour. Men are also five times more likely than women to turn to alcohol and drugs as a means to reduce the feelings of depression. Poor health, anxiety disorders, dysfunctional relationships, overwork and obsessive behaviour are other typical ways male depression may manifest itself.

Friends, family and even doctors may focus on symptoms, like alcohol addiction, rather than the underlying cause. The National Depressive Foundation reports that two out of three people with mood disorders, like depression, do not get proper treatment because their symptoms are not recognized as depression.

4 He Must Be Crazy

Doctors say that many depressed men fail to report their symptoms because of the continuing stigma of mental illness. The organization MIND (National Association for Mental Health) claims that the popular media exacerbate mental-health stigmas by using words like 'loony', 'crackers', and 'nutcase'.

Adding the shame of madness to the stigma of depression may make a depressed man feel doubly humiliated. He may secretly be terrified of hospitalization, shock treatments, loss of control and being unable to make his own decisions. These treatments and repercussions are myths, but to the depressed man they may seem real.

It is important to make a very real distinction between being depressed and being crazy. They are two very different things.

5 Depression is Wilful

The fact that most of us feel depressed from time to time but are able to recover and move on makes it hard for us to empathize with a man who gets depressed and stays depressed. We are likely to be intolerant of his behaviour and perceive it as indulgent, weakness or lack of backbone. We think he should stop feeling sorry for himself. He should pull himself together!

In a recent survey, the US National Alliance for the Mentally Ill (NAMI) found that over 70 per cent of those who responded think that mood disorders are due to emotional weakness. Only 10 per cent knew that mental illness has a biological basis and involves the brain.

The popular belief that with enough willpower and character a man can conquer depression is likely to plunge him even further into darkness and despair. A man is supposed to be in control and keep his personal problems to himself. When he realizes he can't cope anymore, his sense of futility and failure can become even more acute.

You may find that you don't want to address the problem of depression in a man you care about, for fear of hurting his male pride. Unfortunately, colluding with him just confirms his suspicion further that he should be able to snap out of it by himself.

Depression is not wilful. And it's not a way that a man uses to get back at you for some past wrongdoing. Lifestyle changes, willpower and a positive attitude can sometimes alleviate depression. But sometimes they can't. An illness or chemical imbalance in the brain can cause or trigger depression. Depression is not always what it seems. A man can't always 'snap out of it' or cope on his own. He needs sustained help.

6 Talking Won't Help

Talking can help to ease the pain of depression, but men don't, in general, like discussing their feelings.

Experience has taught men that society is not yet comfortable with a man who expresses his feelings. If women reach out to talk about how they feel, they tend to be met with sympathy and nurturing. If men reach out, they are frequently met with hostility and social disapproval, inspiring social awkwardness. Small wonder many men don't have much faith in talking.

Ashamed of looking needy and vulnerable, men tend to let their pain furrow deeper. Asking for help, talking about their problems or having therapy is not the 'manly' thing to do. Men are supposed to 'do', not talk. Many men would rather suffer in silence than acknowledge physical or emotional distress. In extreme cases, some men would rather die than talk about their vulnerabilities.

7 Treatment for Depression Is Addictive

A man may be aware that he needs help, but be terrified of becoming addicted to that help. It takes a great deal of effort to deny, control or hide feelings that hurt. There could be a tremendous fear that once these feelings come out in the open there will be no stopping them, and that repression will be replaced by helpless dependency on therapy and drugs.

Sometimes drugs need to be taken for life, but more often than not treatment is not long term and doesn't become a habit. The main aim of therapy and medication should be to encourage a man to regain a sense of control over his life. It serves its purpose and the man moves on. Treatment for depression should not create a life-long dependency.

8 Depression Is the Same for Everyone

How depression manifests itself will differ from man to man. In some cases it will be totally debilitating. In others it will be hard to tell whether or not he is depressed. Some men may develop conditions alongside depression, like alcohol and substance abuse; others will not.

'Depression' is the term used to describe a wide variety of psychological, biological and genetic elements ranging from temporary unhappiness to suicidal despair. It isn't a single ailment that affects every man the same way.

Just as no two men are exactly alike, each man's experience of depression will be unique. The experience of depression is not the same for every man.

9 Men Don't Worry About Things Like That

At the dawn of the new millennium, as both sexes struggle to redefine themselves, it is becoming apparent that not only are women worrying about things traditionally only thought to concern men, but men are worrying about things traditionally only thought to worry women.

The increasing number of men who are joining women in their obsessive concern about appearance, body image, weight, body shape and size is a case in point. It's estimated that 10 per cent of the 90,000 diagnosed cases of eating disorders that occur every year in the UK are men.

Men are also reacting with greater sensitivity to life events and passages. The issue of having children or not, for instance, or the angst of midlife and accompanying hormonal changes can all have a deep impact on a man's sense of self-worth.

10 You Can't Function Normally If You Are Depressed

Each day may be a struggle, but a man who is depressed can function normally, carry out his responsibilities and lead a productive life. It's a myth that people with depression cannot function. In fact, 72 per cent of depressed individuals are in the workforce. Some are taking medication or some other form of treatment. Many simply carry on despite their deep emotional pain.

It is well known that some of the most productive and creative men suffer from depression. Their work, their relationships or other commitments often act as a lifeline to help them cope with their pain and despair.

Many famous men have struggled with clinical depression, including Abraham Lincoln, journalist Mike Wallace, presenter Dick Cavett, comedians Rodney Dangerfield, Spike Milligan and John Cleese, statesman Winston Churchill, artist Rembrandt, poet Coleridge, actor Rod Steiger and writers William Styron, Ernest Hemingway and Mark Twain.

Letting go of common misunderstandings about how a man should behave won't be easy for either you or him. Be patient, and don't be surprised if from time to time old assumptions resurface. A part of you will always feel that this shouldn't happen to a man. A part of him will always feel that his distress is shameful and should be concealed from others.

Sometimes a man becomes so adept at hiding his pain that it is hard to tell if he is depressed.

The next chapter will help you delineate the symptoms so that you can distinguish between normal sadness and clinical depression. Case histories and authors who have written about male depression will help you learn about the elements of depression, so that you can better understand what he is going through and find appropriate ways to help. And if he is feeling down or blue, and not clinically depressed, you will see why this state of mind shouldn't be ignored, either.

2

Recognizing Depression

Depression is an illness of the feelings.

It is a mood cancer. It can rob a man of his life's worth and make him sicker than most physical illness other than heart disease and cancer.
Gail Sheehy, *Understanding Men's Passages*

The word 'depression' describes many different emotional states, from a simple case of the blues, when a man can still function, to major depression, when he can see only hopelessness and despair, and even bodily functions are affected.

There is a striking loss of zest – the sufferer is stricken with a debilitating lack of interest and drive. Nothing matters.
Anthony Clare, *Depression and How to Survive It*

Is He Depressed?

You may be wondering if the man you know is depressed. The following list will help you if you suspect a man you care about is depressed.
Ask yourself:

Is the man you care about constantly worrying and anxious most of the time?

Has he lost interest or pleasure in everyday activities he used to enjoy?

If you can answer yes to both these questions and to four or five of the questions on the checklist below, the chances are the man you care about is depressed.

- Does he seem tired all the time?
- Does he lack interest in sex?
- Is he acting withdrawn and lonely and talking about being isolated?
- Is he feeling overwhelmed by negative emotions?
- Has the nature of your relationship changed? Has he withdrawn from you or become more dependent on you? Has he started to blame you for his unhappiness? Does he lash out at you for no apparent reason?
- Has he become a bit of a hypochondriac, complaining of mysterious pains that seem to migrate around his body?
- Is it difficult for him to accomplish even simple tasks, like washing, dressing and eating?
- Do you think that he has been crying?
- Does he seem vague, confused and forgetful?
- Is it hard for him to make any kind of decision?
- Are his sleeping habits changing?
- Does he seem restless, panicky and anxious?
- Does he eat less than before? Has he lost weight without dieting?
- Has he suddenly gained weight or is he eating far more than usual?
- Does he appear vulnerable or 'over-sensitive'?
- Is he:
    regularly taking drugs or drinking to the point of losing control?
    behaving badly – lying, stealing, cheating?
    taking more and more time off work or school?
    harming himself by cutting, burning or scratching?
    showing signs of having been harmed by others – unexpected bruising, cuts or burns?

    having bouts of rage or violence?
    having horrible memories of past events?
    hallucinating sights, sounds and smells?
    having periods of frantic energy followed by periods of little or
    no energy?
    having panic attacks or surges of strong anxiety?

- Does he seem sad and pessimistic about himself and the world?
- Does he talk about feeling hopeless, guilty and worthless?
- Does he find it hard to concentrate?
- Is he irritable most of the time – or alternatively, is he unusually placid, which may go so far as physically slowing down in speech, action and thought?
- Does he show a preoccupation with death or suicide?

To summarize, if you notice the following five warning signs for more than two weeks, it is important that the man you care about seeks advice from a mental health professional (Chapter 8 will show you how you can encourage a man reluctant to acknowledge he is depressed to seek help):

constant worrying
emotional instability
loss of sex drive
inability to make decisions
lack of self-confidence.

If your loved one is having suicidal thoughts, it is even more critical that he be seen right away. In a crisis, always take him to a hospital emergency room for immediate attention. Suicide is a very real consequence of depression which cannot be ignored (see Chapter 9).

The Spectrum of Depression

Evidence suggests that if a man is unhappy for a long period of time, this may create a biochemical atmosphere in the body that makes him more vulnerable to heart disease, cancer or other life-threatening conditions. Doctors have a clear idea of what actually constitutes a depressive state, and you will learn about this later in this chapter. As you can see from the list of questions above, however, a wide range of behaviours and feelings can be associated with depression.

Unhappy feelings can follow a spectrum, from 'the blues' to major clinical depression.

The premise of this book is that any sign of depression, from minor to major, is a potential threat to a man's physical and emotional health. The advice given will apply, no matter where on the depressive spectrum the man you care about is.

The Blues

All men go through the blues – also known as dysphoric mood states – with some temporary symptoms of depression, but they usually continue to function normally and recover without needing treatment.

Sadness is a natural reaction to common problems, such as the loss of a loved one, failing an exam, financial setbacks, problems at work, depressing news or unresolved conflicts and disappointments. Sadness linked to a particular event is an entirely normal and temporary phase.

Andrew, age 30, was deeply affected by the murder of two-year-old Jamie Bulger, like most everyone else in Britain. It made him feel incredibly sad and empty. For several weeks he ruminated about how violent, corrupt and terrible the world had become. He wondered what the purpose of little Jamie's life had been. After several weeks, however, other events in Andrew's life began to dominate and his sadness faded.

Sadness for no particular reason is equally common. Sometimes the world just turns grey and a man feels unbearably sad and alone, with a bitter taste in his mouth. This experience, however, may be no more than a passing moment. In time the heaviness lifts through a change in attitude or practical action.

Although he is not technically depressed, when a man is feeling blue he will show signs of mild depression. Whether or not the blues will flow into depression is hard to predict. Much depends on the situation and how a man copes with stress. If painful feelings are not dealt with but are avoided, they may erupt in emotional or physical illness of some kind.

Peter, a 35-year-old production manager, diverted his attention from the pain of his recent divorce by constantly worrying about work. He wondered why his productivity was declining and he couldn't make things happen anymore. Without realizing it, Peter's questioning of his competence and overall self-worth edged him towards a nervous breakdown a few months later.

The blues should be taken seriously when they strike. The way a man handles feelings of unhappiness can increase his risk of developing a more serious depression. For example, avoidance can trigger a descent into major depression. Painful emotions need to be dealt with, not, in the words of John Cleese and Robin Skynner in *Life and How to Survive it*, 'freezed-off.'

On the other hand, difficulties shouldn't be obsessed about either. According to the *New York Times* columnist Daniel Goleman in his book *Emotional Intelligence*, if repetitive thoughts about how sad a man is feeling or how badly he is doing in life crowd his mind, depression is far more likely. Goleman believes that one of the 'main determinants' of whether or not a depressed mood will lift is the degree to which a man worries or ruminates. Constant worrying, it seems, is dangerous.

Is He Depressed, or Just Unhappy?

In her seminal text *Depression: The Way Out of Your Prison*, Dorothy Rowe distinguishes between being depressed and being unhappy. Unhappy people are able to seek comfort, comfort themselves and let that comfort come through to them to ease the pain. 'But in depression neither the sympathy and concern of others nor the gentle love of oneself is available.' Other people may be there, but their compassion can't pierce the wall of depression. 'Depression is a prison' where the depressed man is both the 'suffering inmate' and the 'cruel jailer.'

Clinical depression, or depression as diagnosed by health professionals, refers to a cluster of symptoms that affect a man's feelings, thoughts, behaviour and physical functions. The condition can last for a substantial period of time despite efforts to lift the mood. In fact, the failure of efforts to raise his mood can make a man feel even more hopeless.

According to the fourth edition of the *Diagnostic and Statistical Manual of Mental Disorders* (DSM-IV), the psychologists' diagnostic manual, the criteria for diagnosing depression are that the man has experienced bouts of depression for longer than two weeks, has experienced changes in appetite, sleep and physical activity, and has thoughts of ending his life.

The two-week period during which the symptoms first manifest must represent a change from the man's normal routine, and must cause significant distress or impairment of his social functioning. If a precipitating event has occurred, such as the loss of a loved one, a period of readjustment when symptoms of depression occur is normal. A diagnosis of depression won't be made until symptoms have persisted for longer than two months.

Clinical Depression

The various types of clinical depression are listed below.

Dysthymia

A more serious condition than the blues is low-grade melancholy, 'feeling down' for at least a year. The condition is known as dysthymia (literally meaning 'ill-humoured'), chronic depression, or neurotic depression, and it does not dramatically alter normal functioning.

Chronic mild depression tends to have milder symptoms than major depression, but it can be longer lasting. Whether or not dysthymia is a separate entity from major depression or simply a less intense form of the same disorder remains a subject of debate.

Although dysthymia usually develops before the age of 25, most men are not diagnosed until they reach midlife. Most men with dysthymia claim that they've felt low and depressed for so long they don't remember feeling any other way. 'Doubtless depression has hovered over me for years, waiting to swoop,' says William Styron, who wrote an autobiographical account of his own depression in *Darkness Visible*.

Major Depression, or Unipolar Depression

Major depression is the most widespread form of mental disorder, according to the US National Institute of Mental Health. Major depression impairs a man's functioning. The situation can be life-threatening: men suffering from severe depression may think about taking their own life. Currently, therapists identify three different forms of major depression: melancholic, atypical, and psychotic.

MELANCHOLIC DEPRESSION

Melancholic depression involves symptoms of deep sadness and feelings of lowness and lethargy. Simon, age 18, suffers from melancholic depression. He wakes before dawn, and his mother can hear him silently crying until the alarm clock rings a few hours later. He has college to attend, but rarely gets there. He has no appetite for food or for life, and withdraws from social contact as much as possible.

ATYPICAL DEPRESSION

A man with atypical depression may feel better when life gets more positive. He may enjoy food, sex and his work. He won't lose his appetite or have problems sleeping. On the contrary, he may overeat and oversleep. He tends to be very sensitive to rejection, and panics easily, but apart from that it is very hard to tell he is depressed most of the time. Frustration about the disparity between his gloomy inner state and the productivity of his life can precipitate a crisis.

PSYCHOTIC DEPRESSION

Psychotic depression is the rarest form of major depression. Psychotic men lose touch with reality completely and experience delusions and hallucinations. Psychotic men usually require immediate treatment and hospitalization.

There are also depressions described as 'secondary' because they result from other mental and physical problems. A high incidence of depression, for example, occurs with illnesses like diabetes, cancer, heart disease, stroke and disorders of the brain like Alzheimer's, Parkinson's disease, epilepsy and multiple sclerosis. In the past, doctors tended to think that it was natural for someone suffering from one of these illnesses to feel down because of his condition. They did not see depression as something that also needed to be treated. Fortunately, more and more doctors are recognizing that depression needs to be treated as a separate condition, because it is an illness that can impair recovery.

Manic Depressive Disorder, or Bipolar Affective Disorder

Unlike unipolar depression, where the depressive mood doesn't lift, in bipolar affective disorder a 'down' mood is followed by an 'up' mood immediately or after a spell of stability. At first the highs may seem mild. The man feels energetic, excited, talkative, euphoric. He may suddenly get very active. He moves fast, talks fast, barely eats or sleeps. He is self-confident, bordering on the arrogant. He begins new projects, acts impulsively or recklessly. He may become promiscuous. He is often impatient and may become irritable, agitated and even violent if someone tries to slow him down.

Manic episodes are invariably followed by deep depression. If untreated, the condition could spiral out of control, so that mood changes become more and more frequent, even from hour to hour.

Seasonal Affective Disorder (SAD)

SAD involves periods of depression on an annual basis during the same time each year – beginning most often between the months of October and November, as the days grow shorter, and ending in March or April with the coming of spring. Symptoms include intense food cravings (especially for carbohydrates), lethargy, oversleeping, weight gain and general fatigue during the autumn and winter months. The National Institute of Mental Health estimates that about 10 million Americans suffer from SAD, most of them in the northern part of the country where it stays darker longer.

Conditions that Commonly Co-exist with Depression

More than 43 per cent of people with major depressive disorders have histories of one or more other psychiatric disorders, according to the US Department of Health and Human Services. The most common conditions that occur at the same time as depression include addictive behaviours, eating disorders, anxiety disorders, abusive behaviours and post-traumatic stress disorder.

Alcohol and Drug Addiction

Alcohol and drugs affect a man's brain chemistry, and therefore his mood. Like depression, addiction appears to have a genetic connection, with children of alcoholics more likely to develop an addiction. Also, like depression, addiction appears to involve a disruption of brain chemicals combined with psychological factors.

Many men start drinking or taking drugs to relieve the pain of depression. A vicious cycle can begin. The physical, social and psychological problems caused by substance abuse make a man feel hopeless, weak and sad. More alcohol, cocaine or other substances are needed to lift his mood. It is a morbid cycle of neediness and despair.

My brother started drinking when he lost his job. I didn't realize how addicted he had become until he lost his next job because of his drinking.

Jane

Alcoholism and drug addiction are complex disorders, with complex causes and treatment options. Covering these problems in any depth goes beyond the range of this book. Suffice to say, it is vital that you and the man suffering from the addiction give doctors a complete and honest breakdown of his use of alcohol and drugs.

Other forms of addictive behaviour are commonly associated with depression. Some men are becoming addicted to the internet. For parents worried about their sons spending all night at the computer, the tragic case of Philip Katz is a nightmare warning.

At just 37, Philip Katz, a prominent figure in the world of computers and the internet, died of chronic alcoholism. His death was described as 'a parable of the times'. Here was a man so totally subsumed by the world of computers that he became alienated from family and friends. Shy, lonely and unable to deal with the real world, Katz became addicted to virtual reality and disembodied relationships with a keyboard and a monitor.

Obsessive-compulsive disorder may also co-exist with depression. When obsessive thoughts become severe, a man may change his behaviour in order to cope. He engages in compulsive actions that don't make sense to anyone except himself. Common compulsive acts include continual checking or counting, hand-washing, cleaning or tidying.

Other compulsions include what is known as *bigorexia*, a preoccupation with not being big enough and an all-consuming desire to beef up like a hulk. According to the authors of *The Adonis Complex*, male self-worth is becoming increasingly tied to body image, and the average man has deep insecurities about the way he looks. Weight-training to achieve the ultimate macho physique becomes an obsession.

Looking at men who were much more toned than me left me feeling very inferior about my own shape. It got to the point where I became obsessed with my muscles and constantly worked at refining them.

Dan, 39, health club manager

The compulsion to exercise, perhaps triggered by the endorphins released during aerobic activity, can also occur. A man will spend hours running, swimming or engaging in other forms of aerobic exercise. If he misses a session, he feels anxious and unsettled. Sometimes the compulsive need to exercise can take over a man's life to the extent that his work, his relationships and even his health suffer.

The compulsion to have sex with as many women and/or men as possible, as often as possible, can also be associated with depression, as are the compulsion to work – when a man reaches the point when he can't switch off anymore and engage in activities outside of the workplace – and the compulsion to gamble.

The correlation between depression and various forms of compulsive behaviour is high. It is extremely important for concurrent addictions and depression to be treated together. The combination can trigger deeper and longer depressions.

Eating Disorders

Anthony finds it hard to concentrate on anything. He thinks that his erratic behaviour and muddled thinking are due to the stress of his father's death. His partner, Bruce, thinks he may be bulimic.

Anthony is not alone. It is estimated that up to 75 per cent of eating disorder patents suffer from some sort of major depression.

Most of these will be women, but eating disorders such as anorexia, bulimia and obesity seem to be increasing in incidence in men, according to a 15-year study conducted by Professors Harrison Pope and Katherine Phillips of Harvard and Brown universities, and clinical psychologist Roberto Olivardia.

A concern about health that is taken to the extreme is often the starting point. Bullying and taunts about appearance from one's peer group may also be powerful triggers. Sometimes, though, it is simply a desire to conform to the media image of male desirability. Contrary to popular belief, men do worry about the way they look.

Anorexia involves a distortion in body image and a morbid fear of fat that leads to self-starvation. Although hungry and abnormally focused on food, men with anorexia force themselves not to eat. No amount of logical reasoning will convince a man to break the destructive pattern of reducing his food intake to virtually nothing, weighing himself repeatedly and fearing food. Bulimia, which involves eating vast quantities of food in short spaces of time and then making oneself vomit, is also on the increase for men.

Like depression, eating disorders – including compulsive eating, obesity, anorexia and bulimia – involve a disruption of brain chemistry as well as psycho-social stresses. Treatment usually involves a combination of medication and psychotherapy. It is important that any eating-related problems be discussed with doctors or therapists at the same time that depression is addressed.

Anxiety Disorders

According to the National Co-morbidity Survey, up to a quarter of adult Americans may experience an anxiety disorder in the course of their lifetime. Millions of men experience panic attacks and anxiety disorder in combination with depression.

Panic disorders appear to be present in about 20 per cent of men with major depression, and 30 per cent suffer symptoms of anxiety disorder.

I woke convinced that an earthquake would open up the earth and I would be sucked into an abyss. My stomach churned. Horrific images raced through my mind. Waves of panic seized me.

John, age 63

As with most symptoms that co-exist with depression, it's hard to tell what causes what. In some cases, depression appears to trigger panic attacks. In others, the stress of dealing with panic and anxiety can be so isolating and demoralizing that it causes depression.

Abusive Behaviour

A man may release his hurt by inflicting it upon others, especially those who care about him. There may be verbal outbursts of anger or irritability when he lashes out at you or, worse still, physical violence. Violence is often the male way of releasing pain and feeling better. It is like saying to someone else, 'Now you understand my pain.' This is one of the most terrible aspects of male depression.

I could tell at once when Dad was in one of his black moods. Nothing I could say or do was right. He would hit me for no real reason. I lived in constant fear.

Daniel

On very rare occasions a man may feel so hopeless that he not only attempts to take his own life, but the lives of others, too. Usually it is the lives of those closest to him that are threatened: The family man who kills his family before killing himself, the son who murders his parents and then takes his own life. Depression makes these men feel not just that their own lives but the lives of others are pointless and/or painful. The media are quick to report such ghastly scenarios, but it is important to remember that such instances are very rare.

Other men turn the violence inwards upon themselves. They may engage in self-mutilation; cutting their arm repeatedly with a knife, for instance. Jamie, age 19, has been battling against self-mutilation for seven years. When asked why he cuts himself, he explains that it is 'like releasing all the bad and evil inside. I feel better, relieved, when I hurt myself and see the blood flowing.'

In suicide, the preferred means are often violent. Rather than take a drug overdose, a man is more likely to use a gun, a rope or a knife, or to throw himself in front of a train or from a building.

Post-traumatic Stress Disorder

Most men who develop post-traumatic stress disorder, or PTSD, do so after taking part in military combat, although it can also be a response to disturbing, threatening life events such as rape, sexual abuse, assault or crimes of violence. The stress that it takes to bury horrific memories can trigger a bout of depression. High rates of depression exist in men who were abused in childhood.

....

I don't know why, but I couldn't commit to anyone anymore. I couldn't let anyone close to me. It was when I couldn't stand to be touched and I couldn't sleep or eat that I finally realized I needed help.

William, age 32

....

Symptoms of PTSD include recurrent flashbacks of the event, anger, irritability, nightmares, emotional numbness, difficulty concentrating and depression.

How Does He Feel?

When a man you care about is depressed, it is hard to imagine how he feels unless you have experience of depression yourself.

Roger, age 65, feels that his depression was 'a living death, which robs everything of meaning or purpose. I felt numb.'
Mike, age 46, compares depression to a 'hammer hitting a bruise over and over again'.
Paul, age 37, describes it as 'the gradual shutting out of all light'.
Chris, age 20, told me that it was like 'an all-consuming dark swamp that took over my life'.
For Perry, age 16, 'Every day is a battle to survive.'

Many seriously depressed men say that, forced to choose between depression and a heart attack, they would choose the heart attack.

Spike Milligan told the psychiatrist Anthony Clare, 'It is like every fibre in your body is screaming for relief, yet there is no relief ... The whole world is taken away, and all there is is this black void, this terrible, terrible, empty, aching, black void.'

Dr John Horder, one-time president of the Royal College of General Practitioners, told the magazine *Medical News* that depression felt like 'a form of total paralysis of desire, hope, capacity to decide, to do, to think, or to feel – except pain and misery'.

F Scott Fitzgerald described depression as a 'nocturnal void where the self wages an intimate struggle against hopelessness and despair'.

William Styron declared in *Darkness Visible* that 'loss in all its manifestations is the touchstone of depression ... The loss of self-esteem is a celebrated symptom, and my own sense of self had all but disappeared, along with my self-reliance.'

A depressed man can't see anything in life other than futility, suffering, pain, anxiety, loss, destruction and misery. Emotionally, mentally and physically he feels drained, dysfunctional and defeated.

In some instances, a man may believe he has become such a burden that everyone would be better off if he ended his life. Suicide seems to be the only option left to relieve his suffering.

I have in my possession letters and documents concerning my grand-uncle, Menko Ennen, to whom this book is dedicated. My grandmother frequently wrote to him expressing her concern. In one of his last letters, he told her to 'stop worrying':

I can't bear to have you worrying. I'm really not worth worrying or even thinking about.

Three and a half months later, at the age of 23, Menko put a gun in his mouth and killed himself.

Is It My Fault?

When you learn that a man you care about is depressed, you may wonder if you, in some way, are to blame. Is it something you did? Should you have seen it coming? Are you doing enough to help?

If your relationship has been or is stressful, it is easy to start blaming yourself. Stress is linked to the incidence of depression, but *it is not stress, but how a man chooses to react to stress that can trigger depression.*

Being in a close relationship with a depressed man can leave you feeling that you are in some way connected with the cause of his depression. You may feel that you have failed him in some way. But if you really want to help him, the first thing you have to do is stop blaming yourself.

You are not to blame.

However stormy your relationship may be. However strong your disagreements may be. However you may have behaved towards him, however much stress you may have caused him, however guilty you feel and however guilty he may make you feel, you did not cause his depression.

His depression is not your fault.

What Causes Depression?

In the past 20 years there has been a great deal of research into the causes of depression. Most experts agree that a number of factors – biochemical, genetic, psychological and environmental – work together to trigger depression.

Sometimes a cause can be determined, and the most common are listed below – but bear in mind that in some instances absolutely no precipitating stress or biological predisposition to depression is apparent. Depression can appear for no apparent reason, like a mysterious bolt out of the blue.

Biochemical Explanation

Some researchers believe that depression is linked to endocrine abnormalities. The endocrine system controls the production and functioning of a man's hormones. A disruption of the internal hormonal rhythms associated with light and dark, reduced functioning of the thyroid gland, adrenal gland and parathyroid gland, and fluctuations in levels of the sex hormone testosterone and the stress hormone cortisol have all been associated with male depression.

Improper functioning of certain brain neurotransmitters due to birth problems, heredity or disease may also be the cause. Neurotransmitters are chemical messengers that transmit signals between nerve cells. They control feelings, behaviour and thoughts. Depression is thought to be associated with deficiency in two particular neurotransmitters, serotonin and norepinephrine, but other neurotransmitters, dopamine in particular, are also being studied in relation to depression.

Genetic Explanation

Depression tends to run in families. If a man you care about is depressed, the chances are that he has a relative who also experienced depression. Children of a person with depression are more likely to suffer bouts of depression than those born to parents without depression. Research in Ottawa claims that a faulty gene, affecting serotonin levels in the brain, is associated with depression. This gene is present in twice the number of those who attempt suicide as in the rest of the population. Other research shows that if one identical twin is depressed, the other has a 70 per cent chance of being depressed too.

The American Psychiatric Association believes that depression occurs one to three times more often among those who have a parent, sibling or child who has suffered from depression. Family therapist Terrence Real has written eloquently of the transmission of depression from parents to their sons. The unconscious unresolved suffering that stems from the depression of previous generations operates in families like an emotional debt, according to Real. 'We either face it or we leverage our children with it.'

Environmental and Psychological Stresses

Research shows that major life stresses can trigger bouts of depression. Too much stress can upset the delicate balance of neurotransmitters in a man's brain and thus leave him susceptible to depression. Stress boosts production of the hormones responsible for an increase in breathing and heart rate, muscle tension and anxiety. Prolonged exposure to the chemicals produced under stress can lead to physical symptoms ranging from allergies to impotence to insomnia and muscle pain. It can also lead to the blues and depression.

These stresses can be negative – death in the family, divorce or illness – as well as positive – a new job, marriage or the birth of a child. All life changes, both positive and negative, can cause stress, and stress can upset a man's internal balance.

Other psychological and environmental stresses that have been found to be linked to depression in men include poor communication skills, leading to feelings of loneliness and helplessness, bullying and victimization by peer group, lack of social support, the widespread decline in job security, alcohol and drug abuse, certain medications, poor health, homelessness, physical pain, incapacitating accidents and, especially, terminal illnesses, post-traumatic stress from combat or sexual abuse, the anxieties of the modern world, confusion over gender roles, low self-esteem, unemployment, poverty, debt, frustration in the workplace, personal stress as a result of difficult or broken relationships and bereavement, retirement, and natural disasters.

In *Darkness Visible*, William Styron describes the loss of a parent as 'an insufferable burden of rage and guilt ...', which carries 'the potential seeds of self-destruction'. Neuroscientists are now researching the impact on the brain of early psychological losses such as the death of a parent, abuse or abandonment. Often the stress of such traumas alters the neural pathways, so that subsequent losses – even small ones – remind a man of his original distress and can trigger depressive illness.

What to Rule Out First

If you think a man you know is suffering from depression, it is possible that symptoms of lethargy, hopelessness, anxiety, low self-esteem, changes in his appetite and sleep patterns and so on could be signs of a physical condition requiring a different approach than depression. Before you assume that the man you care about is depressed, it is important that a doctor rules out other possible causes first.

As pointed out earlier, certain conditions such as cancer, heart disease or arthritis, which are chronic and debilitating, an addiction that takes control of a man's life, or a brain or endocrine disorder can all trigger depression in susceptible men.

Many infectious diseases, such as viral pneumonia, hepatitis, tuberculosis, or even a bout of flu can also cause a variety of mood disturbances. Chronic fatigue syndrome has symptoms that closely resemble depression, including low energy, headaches, stomach upsets and a feeling of hopelessness. Acquired Immune Deficiency Syndrome (AIDS) may also have depression-related symptoms. These conditions may cause symptoms that indicate depression, but once the condition is addressed, the depressive symptoms can disappear.

A number of widely used medications have also been implicated in episodes of depression. Drugs used to treat cardiac conditions, anxiety disorders, arthritis and other autoimmune disorders, asthma, cancer and hormonal imbalances list depression among their side-effects. If the man you care about is taking any medication that is causing depression, he may be able to switch to another drug, or lower the dose, or, if that's not possible, his doctor may prescribe antidepressants which interact safely with his current medication.

Recognizing Depression (ask)

It is often hard to tell if a man is depressed, because men in general tend to be less comfortable with verbal self-disclosure than women. Having said this, there are signs you can recognize.

Depression is an *affective* disorder that affects a man's mood, but it will also affect his health and his behaviour. The following description may help you. Bear in mind, though, that depression has many different ways of manifesting itself.

A depressed man will experience low moods from time to time when he loses interest in everyday activities. You may notice that he seems to have lost enthusiasm for activities he used to enjoy. He may have loved sport, for instance, but no longer seems interested. He may have been very fond of his pet dog, but is no longer taking proper care of the animal.

He may also seem anxious, sad, withdrawn, preoccupied or just despondent for longer than normal. Communication and intimacy will be difficult, but if you do get him to talk he could use words like 'bored', 'dreary', 'slow', 'fed up' or 'pointless' to describe how he feels.

A clear warning sign for you to be aware of is a state of constant worry, also known as rumination, when negative, anxious thoughts about his past, present and future stubbornly predominate. You may notice that he seems to be pessimistic about almost everything. He may start talking about a feeling of hopelessness and futility, or of life having no meaning. In severe cases he may even talk about death and suicide. He may tell you that he can't stop this flow of negative thinking.

The depressed man may also have problems thinking clearly and concentrating. He's likely to be forgetful and indecisive. He could become more dependent, though he might deny or try to hide it. He may appear to be constantly on edge and be prone to flying off the handle for no apparent reason. In some cases he may lash out at you or other people. He may blame you for his problems, or tell you he doesn't want you in his life anymore. He may be more disorganized than usual. There may also be an absolute terror and dread, out of proportion to actual events.

....

I feel like I am about to jump from an airplane and nobody has checked that I have a parachute. I'm frightened of just about everything.

Stan, age 23, describing his anxiety
....

Eating habits may change when a man is depressed. He is most likely to eat less, but sometimes he may eat much more. When Michael, age 39, lost his son in a car accident, he found himself incapable of eating. He lost five and a half stone and was admitted to hospital when he was too weak even to get out of bed. Wayne, age 15, on the other hand, gained a massive six stone when his parents separated and he was put into care.

You may notice that he drinks more alcohol than usual, or that he starts smoking more cigarettes. There may also be increased spending and reckless driving.

Other stress signals include habits like finger-tapping, foot-swinging or knee-jigging, or grinding of his teeth in the night. He may also start scratching itches that don't exist, smoothing hair that is already in place, or just keep fidgeting. Facial gestures associated with stress include repeated swallowing, lip-chewing, eye-blinking, lip-clicking or tic-like spasms.

Some men simply tune out from what is going on around them. They hear but don't listen.

Depressed men may also experience a loss of libido. Some, however, have an insatiable need for sexual gratification. If you are in a relationship with a depressed man, it is all too easy to suspect that he is having an affair or losing interest in you sexually, but the real reason may be that his self-loathing is so great that he can't get aroused anymore. Sometimes he may become so obsessed with his health, weight or appearance that obsessive eating and exercising habits take over his life.

Getting a good night's sleep won't be easy for him. He may wake in the early hours of the morning. He may be sleepy all day and wide awake all night. He may not even be able to sleep at all. Should he get to sleep, his sleep will be restless and uneasy, and there may be nightmares. On the other hand, he may sleep much longer than usual. Whatever the case, sleep won't give him relief from the constant fatigue and exhaustion he feels. 'I've got no energy' may become a constant refrain.

His movements may probably slow right down; 'as if he is moving through a jar of treacle' is how one mother described her son's behaviour. You may even notice that his breathing is heavy. His posture will look dejected and he will often shuffle rather than walk. Some men find it impossible to go about their routine, so that even simple tasks like getting dressed defeat them, but others are able to continue functioning with apparent normality.

What Type of Man Gets Depressed?

Depression is certainly a feature of the lives of many complex, sensitive and creative men: Coleridge, Rembrandt, Van Gogh and Ernest Hemingway to name but a few. Some experts even believe that there may be a tragic trade-off between moments of genius and cycles of depression.

Don't be misled into thinking, however, that depression only strikes the more sensitive, creative, introverted, intelligent kind of man. This couldn't be further from the truth. It occurs in men at the bottom end of the social and educational scale, men who are poorly educated and poorly equipped to deal with the dynamics of the modern world. It occurs in men regardless of their social, cultural or educational backgrounds. It occurs in men with ordinary lives and ordinary aspirations. It also occurs in unusually strong-willed, forceful and charismatic men. Winston Churchill, for instance, suffered regular bouts of depression, which he called his 'black dog'.

High achievers, brilliant businessmen and even those who make others laugh as their profession, such as John Cleese and Spike Milligan, are prone to depression. A man may be the life and soul of the party, the last person in the world you would suspect of suffering from depression. But a deep pain may lie beneath a jolly good-for-a-laugh front or an 'I'm in control' attitude.

Certain personality traits may predispose a man to depression. But it is impossible to stereotype or generalize. Deep despair can overwhelm any man, regardless of his personality type, age, intelligence, creativity, financial status or social background. Depression does not discriminate.

There are, however, certain times in a man's life when he is more vulnerable to depression than others, and certain circumstances that increase the risk. It will be helpful if you are aware of them. The next chapter will explore times of special risk for men.

3

Depression:
A Man's Special Risk

In many ways there is no better time to be a man.

Social and educational background no longer restrict earning capacity. Divorce has lost much of its stigma, and men can move away from difficult and stressful relationships. The incredible advances in science and technology ensure flexible and challenging lifestyles. There are tremendous opportunities for growth and change for men today, but along with these opportunities come anxiety about whether or not these challenges can be met, and confusion about what these challenges actually are.

In 1975 journalist Gail Sheehy wrote the groundbreaking book *Passages*, in which she chronicled the life stages decade by decade of men and women in the 1970s. Each stage was pretty clear-cut for men. In the late 1990s, however, Sheehy describes in *Understanding Men's Passages* a completely new set of stages for men:

Today for men the timer of marker events – finishing school, first job, marriage, children, empty nest, retirement, golden years – has turned out to be unpredictable. What a man is supposed to do, and when, is not clear ... Any man who feels a little lost is hardly alone.

Change is inevitable. Many men are finding the new flexibility of the male role challenging and exciting, but others are still struggling to redefine themselves and accept that the old paradigm of male worth through strength, dominance, control and female submission no longer fits into our complex, interdependent world.

Decades of feminism and cultural change have stimulated new demands from women for men to be responsible and intimate equals. Every aspect of a man's life is currently under the spotlight. Patriarchy hasn't been completely overthrown yet, but as Anthony Clare points out in *Men in Crisis*, there is no justification for it anymore, leaving men confused and disoriented about their roles and functions in life.

The days of man the breadwinner and woman the caretaker are well and truly numbered. Virtually everything that a man can do today, a woman can do, too. Women can't see why this should be a problem, but for many men their lives, identities and personalities have always been defined by what a man – and only a man – can do.

Men can no longer pride themselves on being providers; educated and skilled women can provide for themselves. With the decline of heavy industries and the rise of technology, the superiority of male strength is now irrelevant. With the transient nature of the workforce, a man can no longer be sure of a job for life. With the development of assisted reproduction, men aren't even really necessary if a woman wants to start a family.

The roles that traditionally made men feel masculine – provider, protector, authoritarian and father – are all under assault. What role models are there for young men to aspire to? What kind of future is there to look forward to? Is it any surprise that there is an epidemic of suicide among young men?

The truth is that it isn't easy being a man today. In addition, there are also several gender characteristics and personal factors that can increase a man's chances of falling victim to depression.

A Man's Health

A hundred years ago, a man could expect to live longer than a woman. Millennium man has no such advantage. The average man today can expect to live to the age of 72. The average woman lives to be 78. All over the world, women are living between five and seven years longer than men. Unemployed men or men on lower incomes and some ethic groups have a life expectancy of 10 years less than women.

Men are more likely to suffer life-threatening illnesses or be victims of accidents or suicides. Middle-aged men are twice as likely to suffer from heart disease as women, the ever-growing number of overweight men are increasing their risk of health complications, and men are also more likely than women to become addicted to alcohol.

Research shows that four out of five men acknowledge that they take too long to seek medical advice; of those people who don't consult a doctor at least once a year, more than two-thirds are male. Men typically put up with symptoms which could signal serious health problems rather than face the embarrassment of seeing a doctor.

Jim, age 55, is a retired engineer. Jim didn't even visit a doctor when he suffered his first heart attack. He describes the pain as awful, but it passed and he didn't consider it worth seeing his doctor about or mentioning to anyone. Six months later he woke up in the middle of the night in excruciating pain and was rushed immediately to hospital.

The great majority of men master the art of ignoring any health problems, in the firm belief that they will get better on their own. And if they won't consider seeing a doctor for physical pain, they are even more unlikely to see one if the pain is emotional.

One factor in the improved health of women today is their willingness to seek the advice of others when making decisions about their health. Because men don't open up like this, they lack support, which makes it hard for them to decide if what they are experiencing is serious or not. So their attitude towards their health tends to be extreme. Most of the time they ignore it, but in rare cases – like Nigel, age 32, who visits his doctor for every ache and pain at least once a week – they get anxious and obsessed about it. Either way, their health suffers and depression goes untreated.

How Men Feel

There seems to be a built in gender difference. If girls are anxious in a group setting they tend to cower and be quiet, whereas boys respond by running about making a lot of noise. This has mistakenly be seen as boys dominating the space in preschools and so on. However it is actually an anxiety response.

Steve Biddulph, *Raising Boys*

From the earliest age, the differences between men and women begin to show. Men and women are different physically. Their emotional responses differ, too.

The conventional explanation for the problems men have with expressing their feelings is that men are conditioned not to acknowledge them – the 'big boys don't cry' syndrome. But research is proving that the reluctance men have with feelings and with communicating emotion may have a bio-logical root.

This is an area of huge controversy, but some experts believe that a man's capacity to feel is, to a greater degree than in women, physically divorced from his capacity to articulate. The emotional centres of a man's brain are located far more dis-creetly than in a woman's, and the two halves of the male brain are connected by a smaller group of fibres than in the female brain. Information flows less easily from the right (emotional) side to the left (verbal) side, so men tend to have difficulties expressing how they feel.

It's not that he bottles things up – it's more that his brain is not wired as effectively as a woman's for communication and feelings. He feels less comfortable than a woman does talking about his feelings or reaching out for support in times of crisis. And this inclination to withdraw from intimacy and to try and solve his problems alone may well increase the risk of depression.

We'll explore the way men process emotions in more detail later, but for now just be aware that the typical male response to painful and difficult emotions may contribute to a depressed man's sense of isolation, frustration and confusion. He may be able to work things out in his head. He may be able to take the appropriate action. Sometimes, though, he can't cope on his own, and sometimes the action he takes isn't healing, but dangerous. Men tend to turn violence towards others, while women tend to turn it inwards on themselves or, in some cases, on their children.

Furthermore, the instinct to deny, divert or become aggressive simply enables men's anxieties to go undetected or unacknowledged for far longer than in women. And the longer feelings of despair are reinforced, the more likely they are to develop into a downward spiral that is increasingly difficult to resolve without treatment.

Testosterone

Men have considerably more male sex hormones, the androgens, of which testosterone is the most well known, than women.

Testosterone is not just a growth hormone. As well as boosting sex drive, testosterone has been found to help with memory and to provide some protection against heart disease. The hormone is thought to raise the metabolic rate and help burn off unwanted fat. There are claims that it can lower levels of cholesterol, too.

It's helpful to know the typical pattern of testosterone in a man's life. Boy and girl toddlers act more or less the same, but at around four boys receive a sudden burst of testosterone. Somewhere between the ages of 11 and 13, testosterone levels rise sharply, resulting in a sudden growth spurt for boys. By age 14, testosterone levels peak and manifest in pubic hair, acne, strong sexual feelings and general restlessness. By the mid-twenties, the body has adapted to testosterone levels and a man won't usually be quite so reactive. Testosterone gives him a desire to achieve and a surge of creative energy which can be channelled positively. Around the early forties, testosterone levels begin, gradually, to decline. If a man is satisfied with his life achievements, he may feel that he has less to prove.

A few decades ago it was believed that raising testosterone levels in a man could improve his libido and general health, even his mood. But now research is questioning this. High levels of testosterone may be linked with behaviour that increases the risk of poor health and mood. Some experts believe that high levels of testosterone also increase the risk of aggressive and antisocial behaviour, but this is by no means certain. All that can be said with any certainty at present is that the best physical and emotional health is enjoyed by men who have neither too much nor too little testosterone.

No studies have ever proved conclusively that high testosterone equals depression, but certain experts believe that testosterone levels have an impact on a man's mood, behaviour and how he reacts to stress. Professor Shelley Taylor of the University of California, Los Angeles, and senior author of the *Psychological Review*, believes he has discovered a gender difference in the way the sexes respond to stress. According to Taylor's research:

There is one fact we all know about stress – that it triggers the ancient fight or flight response, flooding the body with chemicals, such as adrenaline and cortisol, that help us respond to danger. But with a higher percentage of women now taking part in research projects it appears that the typical female response to stress is different. Instead of fighting or fleeing, women are more likely to 'tend or befriend' – to become more nurturing or to seek support from others, hence the impulse to call a friend.

The key to this behaviour difference is the hormone oxytocin, which promotes relaxation and loving feelings. Both men and women produce oxytocin under stress, but women produce more of it and its effect is enhanced by oestrogen. It is believed by some experts that testosterone puts a brake on the effect of oxytocin, making it harder for men to talk about their feelings and reach out to others when faced with stress.

With a big helping hand from oxytocin, women are less likely to fly off the handle or bury their feelings when confronted with stress. Men are more likely to respond with aggression or denial.

The whole science of gender differences and studies like Taylor's are fascinating, but they are also hugely controversial and outside the scope of this book. Split-brain studies and studies on the role of 'male' and 'female' hormones yield inconclusive results in humans. This tends to surprise most people. Too often they are used as simple excuses for the status quo, when in fact men and women may be more alike than we think. These theories also don't take into account 'neuro-plasticity', the new research showing that chemicals in our brains change according to what we experience.

Researchers at Memorial Hospital in St John's, Newfoundland, discovered that a man's testosterone levels drop by over 30 per cent after the birth of his child. Lower levels of testosterone were associated with the men becoming more parental. If pregnancy can manipulate a man's hormone levels, it is conceivable that being hugged or massaged or spending more time with his children may encourage a man to talk about his feelings rather than bottling them up or lashing out.

A Man's Support Network

Men can lack the emotional support network that women tend to build around themselves. As pointed out, men find it hard to express how they feel, to reach out and to ask for help. As a result they can be more isolated emotionally and socially. This surely has significant implications for their emotional and, some would say, their physical health.

Most straight men tend to have few friends. They have lots of acquaintances, but few intimate relationships. Gay men seem to have a better support network.

A support network consists of family and friends who can give a man emotional support, advice, encouragement, affection and friendship. When there is no social support, and this is combined with poor health or social stress such as unemployment or poverty, the risk of depression increases tenfold.

In his bestseller *The Healing Power of Intimacy*, Dean Ornish has demonstrated that not only can loneliness increase the risk of poor health and emotional problems, loneliness can kill:

While the evidence on the relationship of psychosocial factors to illnesses is controversial, most scientific studies have demonstrated the extraordinarily powerful role of love and relationships determining health and illness.

According to grief expert Mal McKissock, when men shut down their feelings, they slowly begin to die. A bereaved man is eight times more likely to die in the two-year period following bereavement. Failing to feel one emotion, like sadness, can lead to a shut-down of the full spectrum of feelings – anger, fear, warmth and love. Men urgently need to find a way to express their emotions more effectively to avoid negative consequences.

Men do tend to bond through activities like work, and there is a certain camaraderie at the pub or at work or sport, but what these relationships often lack is intimacy and discussion of feelings. Spontaneous outbursts of emotion are still regarded as inappropriate and a sign of weakness. Should a man try to reach out, he may be met with ridicule and victimization, so deeply ingrained is the belief that to be a man you must deny your emotions. A change in attitudes culturally is beginning to take place, but it is slow.

For many men, marriage or a close relationship with a loved woman or man tends to be the lifeline. Research proves that men with close personal relationships lead healthier and happier lives. Single men and men who are divorced or widowed fare worse in the health and survival stakes. Dean Ornish calls attention to the 'healing power of intimacy', which is more beneficial to a man's health than regular diet, exercise, giving up smoking or regular health checks.

Men don't help themselves by neglecting the world of relationships and avoiding emotional intimacy. Many choose to bind their entire identity to their work. They give themselves to their companies or their jobs. The tragic wrong-headedness of this approach is illustrated by the all-too-frequent scenario of the middle-aged man who has given his all to his company and suddenly finds himself redundant. With his day no longer planned out for him by work, and with few friends to support him, he may well ask if this is all there is. If he has a wife and family, his wife has often developed her own social life during his many absences, and his children have grown apart from him. He gave his life to his job, but his job didn't give him a life.

If outside interests, a support network and self-esteem have not been established outside the workplace when a man retires, loneliness, boredom and lack of direction may well trigger a bout of depression.

His Social and Economic Circumstances

Men from all walks of life, young or old, gay or straight, black or white, rich or poor, married or single, suffer from depression. But statistics show that certain groups of men are more at risk than others.

Men over 65 are certainly more at risk. Up to a quarter of all suicides are from that age range. However, in recent years the death rate from suicide in men under the age of 25 is starting to exceed that in older men.

The highest rates of suicide are among men living on their own (or divorced), often employed, poorly educated, homeless, poor and leading rootless lives. Alcohol is an especially dangerous significant factor.

Recent studies suggest that the post-Second World War generation is currently at greatest risk. Researchers theorize that depression in many baby-boomers may be a reaction to the emotional disruptions of growing up in the 1950s and 1960s in the UK and the US, with unprecedented rates of divorce and relocation leading to losses of family, friends and community. In addition, the baby-boom generation came of age in a time of record economic expansion which created great expectations of wealth and success. But their enormous numbers also meant unprecedented competition for schools, jobs and housing, leaving many dreams unfulfilled. The risk of depression increases when there is a gap between what you hoped for and what you actually get. Unfulfilled expectations cause disappointment, frustration, loss of self-esteem and, sometimes, depression.

But those who do achieve their dreams are by no means immune to depression. The high achiever who achieves more than the norm is also particularly susceptible to depression, because making a mark, not building up inner resources, has been his priority.

His Emotional Framework

Some men, because of their biochemical and genetic makeup, are more vulnerable to depression than others. A history of depression in the family should be taken into account, as should early psychological losses like the death of a parent, abuse or violence.

If a man has spent his formative years in care, is homeless, is unemployed, has learning difficulties, feels trapped by poverty, has lived in an abusive household, has a chronic medical condition, a history of sexual abuse, or is addicted to alcohol and drugs, his chances of experiencing depression increase. Stressful social and economic circumstances, such as the loss of job and financial security – many men measure their self-esteem according to their work status – are just as likely to trigger depression as are grief and disappointment when a loved one dies or a relationship splits up.

If a man feels alone, rejected or abandoned, for whatever reason, this could predispose him to depression. But why is it that some men respond to life's stresses with resilience and a sense of purpose and optimism, while others lose their focus?

Perhaps the severity of the stress is the key. Perhaps he has a genetic and biochemical vulnerability to depression. Or perhaps it depends on his constitution.

When life is out of control, does the man you care about see this as a temporary setback that will add to his store of knowledge, or does he see it as a dangerous threat? Does he meet obstacles with anticipation and optimism, or negativity and anxiety? Does he adapt well to change? How does he react under stress? Does he keep calm in a crisis, or is he likely to fly off the handle? Every man faces obstacles, stresses and challenges in his life, but some methods of coping will predispose a man to depression.

His sense of self-esteem is also significant. The value a man places on his competence and sociability may well have an impact on his emotional health. Does he feel that he is taken seriously? Does he feel that his role in the family and/or community is an important one? Does he feel good about his appearance?

Cultural expectations of what it means to be a man also play a part. If a man feels he can't live up to these expectations, or that these expectations don't appeal to him, the result can be depression.

Much will also depend on how he was parented. Did his parents give him comfort, support and encouragement? Did they focus on his strengths? If they focused on weaknesses instead, the chances are he will be more vulnerable to feelings of low self-esteem, and thus to depression.

Think about the man you know. Are there aspects of his life, his coping style, his personality, his self-esteem, his support network, his economic and social circumstances, that make him more susceptible to depression?

His Passages Through Life

Difficult issues for men include: emotional reticence, competitiveness, aggressive tendencies and loneliness. But another factor that always needs to be taken into consideration is a man's age. It can be helpful for you to know the times, or crisis points, in a man's life when his risk of depression increases.

Crisis points can affect a man's growth and development. They do not *cause* depression. Depression only occurs if the crisis is not dealt with in a positive manner. Remembering that each man's life path is unique, and this is only a generalized pattern, let's review a man's life in typical stages.

Boyhood

Increasingly, depression is occurring earlier and earlier in life. Like depression in adult men, depression in childhood is often unrecognized and untreated because the depression is hidden. Children who are depressed don't always appear sad.

In young boys, typical symptoms of depression include:

- lack of interest in things previously important
- negative self-image
- disruptive behaviour in school – 'macho' behaviour, restlessness, disobedience, playing truant, bullying
- aggressive behaviour towards family, other people, animals and objects
- separation anxiety
- changes in eating and sleeping habits
- violent outbursts of temper
- physical complaints without any just cause
- certain learning difficulties, including attention deficit disorder
- antisocial behaviour and isolation from peer group
- a withdrawn and sad demeanour
- apathy or hyperactivity.

According to Steve Biddulph, author of *Manhood* and *Raising Boys*, from the age of six until the age of 14 boys are 'locking on' to a male role model, usually their dad. They are studying how to be men. Boys may wet the bed, steal, act aggressively or develop any number of problematic behaviours if they don't have positive male role models.

Seeking help for depression-prone children at an early age can avert severe depressive episodes later. Severely depressed teenagers often display in boyhood certain behavioural traits such as aggressive or antisocial behaviour. Research is proving that depressive illnesses often first show themselves in child-hood or adolescence. If a boy's parents are unresponsive or abusive in the first few years of his life, some experts believe that his brain may undergo certain changes which make him susceptible to depression.

Adolescence

According to Gail Sheehy, author of *Understanding Men's Passages*, it takes longer to become an adult today than ever before. Adolescence used to span the ages of 14 to about 21, when a man would have left school, started a career and be starting a family. Today boys hit puberty earlier, and often delay decisions about career and relationships until their mid- to late twenties or even their late thirties.

Adolescence is the period when a boy strives to separate from his parents, establish his own identity, become comfortable with his sexuality and think about what kind of life he wants to lead. With so much going on emotionally and physically, it is small wonder many teenage boys get anxious and depressed.

The extension of adolescence that is apparent today means that all the angst accompanying these changes is prolonged. Judging by suicide rates, the transition from boyhood to manhood is a time of great vulnerability to depression. Suicide is now the second leading cause of death among young men (after accidents). More important than ever in this stage is the role of male mentors from the community.

Teenage boys who are depressed often complain that nobody understands them. They may seem restless or irritable, or they may withdraw into their rooms for hours, playing music or surfing the internet. Others fall behind at school or get involved in dangerous activities. Some stop caring about how they look. Others get obsessed about how they look. Frequently they are hard to communicate with.

All these behaviours, in a less extreme form, are normal signs of an adolescent's growing need for independence. The trouble is that any accompanying depression can be easily overlooked until the boy chooses the ultimate form of attention-grabbing action and attempts suicide.

If a boy's family is isolated and antisocial, a boy may try to break out into the world and establish his independence in risky ways. He may fight endlessly with his parents. He may join a peer group that exposes him to the dangers of alcohol, drugs, crime and sexual promiscuity. Attempting to find structure and direction, he could be vulnerable to cult-like organizations, or gang membership.

If a boy can't find a community, he may try to create his own. Unfortunately, though, the friendship patterns among adolescent boys offer little emotional support. If there is bullying he may suffer incredible anxiety, made worse by the fact that he's unlikely to tell anyone about it for fear of being a labelled a 'wimp' or a 'grass'.

A common response to the angst of adolescence is resistance to authority, and this can lead to violent behaviour. There may also be an increase in perfectionism, as he tries to be the perfect student or pupil. The drive for perfectionism is one of the biggest risk factors for depression and suicide, as well as for eating disorders. Perfectionism stems from a desperate desire to take control in a world that seems to be uncontrollable, to find a role in a world that is giving men no clear role. Up to 86 per cent of all eating disorders begin before the age of 20.

....

I couldn't control what my parents thought of me. But I could control what happened to me. I would get high grades. I would be the captain of the football team. I would be popular. That I could decide until I felt empty again and would have to eat loads and throw it all up. I'd feel like a real failure and say I'd never do it again, but sure enough a week later I'd be vomiting again.

Samuel, age 17
....

Starting or leaving college or university is a time of high risk for boys. Student suicides have almost doubled in the UK in the last decade, from 80 in 1990 to 140 in 1998. This could be put in the context of a rapidly expanding and diversifying student body, but according to new research carried out by the University of Chichester, contributory factors include the break-down of their parents' marriage – many couples split after their children leave home – which leads to students returning to university depressed. Debt is often another trigger. But on the surface there is little linking the individual deaths, except that the young people are often high achievers from supportive families. While appearing to have everything to live for – to everyone else, at least – they decide they can no longer cope with reality and the expectations upon them to succeed. 'We had no idea there was anything wrong' is the most common response from relatives and friends.

It can be hard to tell if a teenage boy is depressed or just being a typical teenager. This isn't made any easier by the fact that an adolescent boy with mood and behaviour problems is often the hardest of all to reach out to. But as you will learn later, the worst thing you can do with young men who are depressed is leave them alone and hope they will sort them-selves out.

Look for problems at school, an inability to bounce back after disappointments or any sudden change in mood that doesn't make sense. Remember, depression in teenagers is often cloaked in so-called 'predictable' teenage behaviour. Episodes of anger are typical, but persistent anger or disruptive behaviour is not. Complaints and behaviour taken to the extreme are warning signs. When teenage boys frequently get involved in crime, smash the car, get drunk or violent or abuse drugs, it could be a sign of depression. Don't ignore these warning signals.

Becoming a Man

We are told it's a man's world, but statistics and recent studies suggest otherwise ...

- Men live an average of five to seven years less than women.
- Up to 90 per cent of violent crimes are committed by men.
- Up to 90 per cent of inmates in prison are men.
- Boys suffer up to 90 per cent of the behavioural problems reported in schools.
- Up to 80 per cent of children with behavioural difficulties are boys.
- Approximately 60 per cent of all adults who abuse alcohol and drugs are men.
- Men are failing in close relationships. The divorce rate is close to 50 per cent, and 70 per cent of these are initiated by women.
- Common health problems for men, like heart attacks, are associated with loneliness and stress.
- Men attempt suicide four times more frequently than women.

For most men, life begins to take a more definite shape sometime in their late twenties and thirties. The thirties tend to be a crucial decade of decision-making about careers, relationships and having children. In the words of Gail Sheehy in *New Passages*, 'Today the turbulent thirties marks the transition to First adulthood.'

Making decisions about career and family life in the thirties can create intolerable pressure and a sense of failure in those vulnerable to depression.

Joe is 31. He has just moved into his sister's house after spending the last two years touring as a drummer with a band. He has started looking for a job in the music business. He thought he could teach or even go into journalism. He wasn't unduly worried. Then suddenly, after a bout of food poisoning, he started to get panic attacks. He would tell his sister that he

was going to look for a job, but would go back to bed after she had left for work.

When a man hits 30, he often finds that pressure really is on him to grow up and make his mark in the world. Leading a rootless life and flitting from one job to another may have seemed exciting and carefree in his twenties, but in the thirties it starts to get jaded. Many thirty-something men get the 'I should have by now' dilemma.

It wasn't that I thought I should have my own business, a car and a house. It's just that I thought I would be established somehow. I certainly didn't think that I'd be single, jobless, in debt and still thinking about what I should be doing with my life. What the hell did I do in my twenties?

Patrick, age 37

On the other hand, a man may feel that he is making his mark, but feel anxious and sad about other aspects of his life. He may not be doing work that he believes in. He may not be working at all. The need to achieve seems to be universal among all adults, male or female. However, the stresses that men encounter along the way to achievement tend to be different. Men tend to be more competitive and to identify with their work more than women, which sets men up for an identity crisis when work is non-existent or breaks down.

He may be unhappy about the state of the country and the world he lives in. He may long for spiritual strength and harmony. He may not feel comfortable or fulfilled about his sexuality. He may not have a partner, and long for one. If he has a partner, the relationship may not be fulfilling. Whether he is gay or straight, the issue of commitment to one particular person may loom large.

He may feel anxious about the prospect of fatherhood, or about the possibility he may never have children.

....

I want children soon. Really because it feels like something to do at my age. I want to be a dad like everyone else. I think having children is what makes you a man. The trouble is, my girlfriend doesn't want to take a career break.

Martin, age 35

....

Anxiety at the prospect of dwindling child-bearing years is not confined to the female species. The image of Bridget Jones' search for Mr Right is beginning to be replaced by the single man who wants to have children. If the trend continues for women to postpone having children, or not to have children at all, the single, broody thirty-something man looks set to become a feature of contemporary life.

Should a man become a father, the awesome responsibility can cause considerable stress.

A surprising number of men get postnatal depression. According to research by Dr Simon Lovestone and Professor Raj Kumar at the Institute of Psychiatry in London, 25 per cent of men suffer depressive symptoms after the birth of a child.

Jack, age 36, said he spent three years trying to bury his emotions when his daughter was born. He felt 'indifferent' to his daughter, hated the drudgery of early childhood, and was resentful of the restrictions it placed on his life. 'It felt like life was all over.' Jack also felt inadequate about his ability to provide for his family.

Society expects much from men today when they become fathers. They are expected to provide for their family and be actively involved in childcare. Getting the tough/tender balance with children right can be incredibly stressful.

Being a father can be one of the most rewarding experiences in a man's life, but it can also be one of the most difficult and demanding. The increased stress levels of parenthood may well serve to upset the mental and physical well-being of some men, and predispose them to depression.

We don't know how to measure the stress that children place on the average man, but one thing is certain: single mother-hood is on the rise, and has been since the 1980s. Daunted by the prospect of family responsibilities, millions of men find that they can't or won't rise to the challenge of fatherhood.

Unresolved emotional problems from the past may also resur-face to haunt a man as he enters adulthood. If a man has been depressed before, he is more susceptible to it occurring again as a reaction to a negative event. So it is important to watch for warning signs. Depression, left untreated, tends to recur.

There may have been violence or abuse in his childhood, and the stress that it takes to bury these painful memories may cause depression. There may also be unresolved issues with parents and loved ones. Many men feel deeply inadequate about themselves because of a lack of emotional intimacy with those they love – not least with their own fathers.

Some father-hungry men embody a secret despair they do not even mention to women. Without actually investigating their own personal father, and why he is as he is, they fall into fearful hope-lessness, having fully accepted the generic diminished idea of father. I am the son of defective male material, and I'll probably be the same as he is.
Robert Bly

The Forties

The hormone production levels are dropping, the head is balding, the sexual vigor is diminishing, the stress is unending, the children are leaving, the parents are dying, the job horizons are narrowing, the friends are having their first heart attack, the past floats by in a fog of hopes not realized, opportunities not grasped, women not bedded, potentials not fulfilled and the future is a confrontation with one's own mortality.

Dr M Lear (reported by Brim, O G, 'Theories of the Male mid-life crisis', *Counselling Psychologist* 6 [1976]: 2–9)

Depression was cited by more than two-thirds of doctors in a recent Gallup poll as the most common emotional problem of middle-aged men. Yet fewer than a quarter of men queried said they would see a doctor if they were depressed.

Chances are a man has lived half his life by the time he reaches forty. The realization that he is not going to live for ever and that where he is now is not where he thought he'd be, or where he wants to be, can strike at any time, but when it happens in the forties it can strike with real urgency and a sense of finality.

There is depression, anger, frustration and rebellion. The crisis is a pervasive thing that seems to affect not just the physical but also the social, cultural, spiritual and occupational parts of man's life.

Jim Conway, *Men in Midlife Crisis*

Many men in their forties feel that they have set their life course and there is little opportunity for change. This is not entirely their fault. Our youth-obsessed culture encourages men to feel that their value decreases with age. At 40 a man crosses an age barrier that influences the way he is viewed at work, by his family and by society in general.

When I missed the promotion I knew I had my last chance to play with the big boys. I'm no longer a high flyer in the company's eyes. More of a hanger-on.

Nick, age 44

Getting older also has an impact on men's sex lives. Recent surveys in the US, led by Professor Panos Zavos, confirm what many have long suspected: Men in their fifties have a third of the fertility of those in their twenties, and make love three times less often. This means that career men who put off having children have less chance of becoming fathers. Older men tend to 'go off' sex, and experience a drastic decline in fertility.

Loss of potency in the boardroom and in the bedroom can cause confusion and low self-esteem. The man approaching midlife has strange and difficult times ahead of him. He may be able to redefine himself and negotiate the way ahead with skill and ease, but many men in midlife stumble.

This deep sense of crisis and failure can lead to unpredictable moods and behaviour.

I believe my husband is either having a breakdown or going crazy. He was always such a reliable, satisfied, solid person with a good sense of humour and of duty. Now his personality has completely changed. All he does is rebel and attack.

Sarah, speaking about her husband of 20 years

The forties are a time of high risk for relationships. Men may walk away from their wives and their families into the arms of another, usually younger, woman or man. It can be a time of potential career disruption or total lifestyle change. Fast cars, motorbikes and trendy clothes may become appealing. Travel may be on the agenda again. For some men in midlife, the panic is so great that it can trigger an addiction. Tristan started to drink heavily in his early forties. 'Alcohol was a part of his life, but when he hit 40 it became his life,' says Tristan's father, Julian.

A man's evaluation of his life accomplishments, hopes and dreams in his forties will decide whether his life ahead is an exciting challenge or a demoralizing drudge. In either case, the sense of crisis and vulnerability that often accompanies this evaluation increases the risk of depression.

Andropause

The medical establishment has long refused to accept that the male equivalent of menopause exists. But more than 50 years' worth of scientific evidence shows that reduced activity of the hormone testosterone can have huge effects on a man's health and potency. Duncan Gould and Richard Pety of the Wellman Clinic in London have suggested that declining testosterone levels produce symptoms not dissimilar to the menopause in women – fatigue, increased perspiration, absent-mindedness, irritability, low mood, premature ageing and loss of libido.

The midlife crisis may overlap the so-called male menopause, but experts like Dr Malcolm Carruthers (author of *Maximizing Manhood: Beating the Male Menopause*) are quick to point out that they are equally separate and distinct conditions.

The midlife crisis is usually confined to the ages of 35 to 45, while the male menopause happens between the ages of 45 and 55. The midlife crisis tends to be triggered by a dramatic event in a man's life, like losing a job or a parent dying. The signs of ageing are more certain during the male menopause, forcing a man to come to terms with his own mortality. This 'male menopause', which Carruthers terms the *andropause*, is a biological event involving declining androgen hormone levels. But even though they are two separate events, both the midlife crisis and the male menopause are times of high risk of depression in men.

Just a few decades ago, reaching 50 did mark the beginning of the end of a man's life. But this isn't the case today. Millions of men reach new levels of power and confidence as they get older. Drawing on the insight, wisdom and maturity that have been gained over the years, they find new goals and opportunities. For many men, the second half of their lives is infinitely richer and more satisfying than the first. Much depends on a man's constitution and attitude, but it is worth bearing in mind that, although the midlife crisis and the andropause don't necessarily *cause* depression, they do set up certain vulnerabilities, both physiological and psychological, to depression.

Depression in the Older Man

'My father seems depressed lately,' says 29-year-old Robert about his 66-year-old father, Richard. 'Ever since Mum died he has found it hard to make things happen. I think everything has caught up with him now. He feels old and alone.'

Richard isn't alone. According to the National Institutes of Health in the US, about 6 million of the 32 million Americans aged 65 and older suffer from some kind of depression. Depression in older men is marked by confusion, disorientation, memory loss, difficulty concentrating, inattentiveness and distractibility. It can be triggered not just by bereavement, but by a sense of loss – loss of purpose, status and a man's role in the family and in society in general. Older men may become apathetic, no longer enjoying activities that once gave them pleasure.

The risk of suicide in elderly men with untreated depression is enormous. When men move into their sixties, the suicide rate soars. According to a 1996 US Federal study, the leading cause of suicide is depression, followed by alcohol abuse, social isolation and physical illness, all of which are associated with depression.

After 60 the hormone levels decline, health is more vulnerable, and palliatives that may have been tolerated by the body, like alcohol, can't be tolerated so well anymore. Coping strategies which may once have kept depression at bay, like work or sport, are no longer relevant. The end of a man's working life often results in loss of status, loss of relationships with work colleagues, and the absence of the social network that had been provided by work.

Only recently has depression in the elderly been widely recognized as a serious concern, and there remains a lack of knowledge about it among the general public as well as the medical profession. At least 50 to 75 per cent of elderly men with depression go undiagnosed.

In an elderly man who is otherwise healthy and lucid, signs of depression are easier to detect. It becomes much more problematic when some form of dementia such as Alzheimer's is present. Up to 50 per cent of elderly people experience both depression and dementia, and both conditions need to be treated. Other medical conditions common in old age, like heart disease, brain injuries, strokes and Parkinson's, also cause depressive symptoms. Careful analysis and diagnosis by a doctor are necessary to determine the cause of a man's changed behaviour.

Part of the problem stems from a misunderstanding of the ageing process. Most of us think of poor health, illness, slowing up, fatigue, low energy levels, irritability and mood disturbances as part of the ageing process. We often think it's natural to feel sad and withdrawn as you approach the end of your life.

The truth is, however, that a man's personality may mellow, but it does not change as he ages.

Many older men can develop new interests and new social lives. Yet the transition from one stage to another can be difficult, as there are few cues for men who are older and little knowledge of how to react when facing a major life change. Many men currently in their sixties, seventies, eighties and beyond are holding on to the value system of their generation, when a man was expected to cope, and asking for help with his feelings was unheard of.

If the elderly man you care about has always been optimistic and outgoing and suddenly becomes quiet and withdrawn, he may be depressed. It's going to be a struggle, though, to get him to seek help. Many men turning 70 or older firmly believe that depression is 'all in the mind' and not a proper illness. They are so convinced of this that they may actually develop physical symptoms, like an upset stomach or headaches, which are actually psychological in origin.

Sometimes the line between depression and typical reactions to predictable life passages can be hard to see, but the information given at the end of Chapter 2 on how to recognize depression should help you delineate the symptoms. Above all, remember that it is never normal to feel unhappy day after day, whatever age a man is.

Recognizing depression in the man you care about is the first and possibly the most important step you as the helper can take. Gather as much information as you can. Get the facts. Read case histories and real-life stories. If you can, talk to medical experts. Recognize how common the condition is, and that you are not alone in your concern. Later in this book you'll learn how your knowledge and awareness of the condition may well be the determining factor in how the man you care about seeks help.

4

The Impact on You

Relationships are like a dance, with visible energy racing back and forth between partners. Some relationships are the slow, dark, dance of death.

Colette Dowling

At the height of my boyfriend's depression I didn't pay much attention to my own life. My world shrank. My work suffered. My health declined. All the responsibilities fell upon me. I felt desperately tired. I knew he wasn't well and I felt sorry for him – but after two years I also resented him.

One particular memory stands out. One morning I arrived at work as usual and was asked to type up an assignment. I simply couldn't get it right. I spent five hours on one simple document. When the document was requested and it wasn't ready, I simply burst into tears, put on my coat, and went home.

The next day I knew an explanation was expected of me. 'Theresa, what is going on?' I couldn't reply. What *was* going on? Even to me, my behaviour seemed out of character. It didn't occur to me that I was feeling so unhappy because of the impact of my boyfriend's depression on me.

I wasn't able to offer an explanation, and simply reassured everyone that it would never happen again. They probably put it down to PMS! For several months the incident hung over me like a cloud and people treated me very carefully, but in time it was forgotten.

Looking back, I now understand how much I was being affected. How hard it was for me to survive each day. How out of my depth I was. How much I needed to be understood. How much of his pain I was absorbing.

The specific details may be different, but if you are in a relationship with a depressed man, you will also be affected.

You want to help, but you are having reactions to the depression yourself. Uncertainty seems to have taken over your life. You have no idea whether he will get better, get worse or, in severe cases, harm himself or others. There is a deep sense of regret that your life seems so abnormal, and a sense of loss that his depression has taken away much of your enjoyment of life. There will be great sorrow, but this will also be mingled with anger and resentment. As much as you care for him, at times you'll feel trapped, burdened down and frustrated.

Depression is a difficult illness for a man to endure, but it can also be difficult for you. Many scientific and medical studies have researched how family and friends are affected by a depressed individual. All these studies come to a similar conclusion: When someone you care about is depressed, it influences all areas of your life. You may be affected emotionally, economically, socially and, sometimes, even physically. Put simply, your whole world turns upside down.

Your Emotions

Research shows that the emotions you may experience include fear, anxiety, frustration, anger, worry, grief, guilt, shame, irritation, resentment, embarrassment, confusion, hopelessness, concern, worry, disappointment, isolation, regret, a sense of burden, uncertainty, panic and depression. Don't think that experiencing such a range of conflicting feelings is unusual. An intense emotional reaction is totally normal, even anticipated, by mental health experts.

From my conversations with caregivers, four responses stood out: disorientation, stigmatization, loneliness, and chronic anxiety.

Disorientation

I don't have control over my life anymore. Whether I have a good or a bad day depends on how he is feeling.

Sandra, whose partner Brian has been depressed for nine years

When a man you care about is depressed, you may feel disoriented for the great majority of the time. It will be hard for you to organize your life, so much depends on the unpredictability of his feelings. Feeling that your life is out of control and that you are overwhelmed by his depression is common.

Stigmatization

When I was asked to explain my reasons for resigning I just couldn't bring myself to tell them that my husband was depressed and I couldn't cope anymore. I felt ashamed.

Sasha, age 47

The stigma surrounding depression can embarrass you; others, not knowing what to say or do, may feel too apprehensive to mention the subject. So the subject is never raised. Friends and family may withdraw from you both and be unwilling to help or, if they do help, the help is given reluctantly.

On the other hand, others may make insensitive comments or, in the guise of wanting to help the depressed man, give unwanted advice or criticize or blame you. Amanda, whose partner Luke suffers from depression, found the criticism from Luke's mother of the way she handled the situation most unwelcome. 'I couldn't believe it. I was trying so hard to cope, and she just made things worse.'

Mood disorders still get a very negative press. Very few people are sensitive to the real issues involved, and the more you yourself believe in these prejudices and misunderstandings, the more stigmatized and isolated you will feel.

Loneliness

I don't think anybody can fully understand how isolating depression can be. Our house used to be one of laugher and noise. Now there is a deafening quiet, broken only by sighs and yawns.

Martin, whose son Neil suffers from depression

If you were once very close to the depressed man in your life, you will miss the intimacies you once shared. It's easy to believe that no one can really understand how wretched your situation is. You may be frightened to leave him alone for long periods. Your social life may quickly disintegrate.

If you reach a point when you feel trapped by his depression, your own anger, frustration and resentment can not only make you depressed, but also isolate you even further from friends and family. Isolation can create almost intolerable stress.

Chronic Anxiety

I have a permanent knot in my stomach. I'm anxious whenever the phone rings. I'm anxious at work. I'm anxious at home. I get so nervous when I drive that I have to stop and take deep breaths.

Rachel, whose partner Steve suffers from depression

When you are feeling isolated, stigmatized and disoriented by the unpredictability of depression in a man you care about, it's small wonder that your anxiety levels will also increase. However positive and optimistic a person you are, being in a relationship with a depressed man is tremendously stressful. You may even find that the anxiety makes you depressed yourself.

Is Depression Contagious?

According to certain American psychologists, depression is indeed contagious. Like tired people who trigger yawning fits in others, depression is apparently like psychological flu. Those who suffer from it spread it to others.

Dr Thomas Joiner, editor of *The Interactional Nature of Depression*, believes that family, friends and colleagues can all pass on the depression bug. It doesn't matter how positive a person you are, if you spend enough time with someone who is depressed, you too are going to suffer anxiety and depression.

Even with strangers or acquaintances – people you are not emotionally involved with – depression rubs off and you pick up 'bad vibes'. In the workplace, for instance, if one member of the team is in a bad mood, it tends to bring down everyone's morale.

The more a man is depressed, the more he spreads his mood to others. For instance, when a husband is depressed he is no longer emotionally available to his wife. She becomes hostile and stressed because she has to take care of the children and do all the things her husband used to do. She herself becomes depressed because of the burdens placed on her. She may even believe it is her fault her husband is down. However, it is *not*. It is important to remember this.

The situation can become a vicious circle – partners going round and round blaming each other for their black moods.

When a man gets depressed and starts showing all the symptoms of irritability for no reason, inevitably his partner suffers. Family members may walk around on eggshells trying not to cause any more problems. They may even retreat into themselves, and inevitably start to blame themselves. If the situation continues for too long, both the depressed man and his family members may need treatment.

Lucy's situation was typical. Her father suffered from recurrent depression:

I felt like I was walking on a tightrope. I had to tread so carefully. He was so bitter, so disappointed all the time. I was constantly trying to support him and encourage him, but giving all the time and receiving nothing back eventually wore me down.

Lucy felt that she had reached the limits of her ability to understand and be compassionate with her father. Witnessing his distress affected her ability to help him. It wasn't easy for her to acknowledge that the situation made her feel angry, frustrated, hopeless and depressed too.

The next time you catch yourself saying, 'Affect me? I don't see how it can affect me. He's the one with the problem,' the chances are you are not recognizing or acknowledging your own feelings and reactions. But, as Part 2 will show you, you don't have to get depressed or physically ill when a man you care about is depressed. Depression does not have to be contagious. There are specific strategies you can use to look after yourself while he is depressed and to help you feel better at the same time.

Your Economic Situation

The emotional impact of depression in a man you care about is huge, but another immediately recognizable impact – especially if you are the partner or parent of a depressed man – is financial.

He may be unable to work because of his condition. If you are in a relationship with him and dependent on him financially, you may feel – like Peggy, whose husband stopped working because of his depression, when they had five children to support – that life has become a 'desperate struggle for survival'.

Or you may find that your fear and concern over his condition is affecting your own efficiency, focus and motivation at work. He may require constant supervision and vigilance. Albert found it impossible to concentrate on anything at work when his son attempted suicide. 'My anxiety levels reached such a high point. I decided to resign before I was fired for incompetence.'

Depression can cause unpredictable behaviour, and some depressed men may suddenly become lavish and impulsive in their spending habits, leaving domestic bills unpaid. Depending on your relationship with him, before you know it you and your family could be in debt.

You may be fortunate and get the cost of treatment or hospitalization paid for you, but you may also find yourself working harder and harder to pay never-ending medical bills. In the US the cost of medication and therapy for depression can be huge, especially if there is no adequate insurance. And even in the UK, where treatment is free on the NHS, long waiting lists may force you to seek and pay for help privately.

If you are struggling financially, there are ways for you to ease the burden which will be detailed in Part 2. For now, be aware of how his depression may be affecting your economic situation and the amount of commitment you give your job or other responsibilities.

Your Relationship with Him

Your connection with the depressed man will also undergo changes. Whether he is your partner, son, brother, father or friend, you are likely to feel repercussions from his condition. But the nature of these effects may differ depending on the type of relationship you have with him.

Regardless of whether or not you live together, it's devastating for you to witness his apathy, disinterest, sadness and constant anxiety. Few people realize the extent to which depression distorts relationships. If a man isn't comfortable with himself, he can't be comfortable with others.

Depression places a huge strain on relationships and can lead to a downward spiral so that both of you end up depressed. Thankfully, mental health researchers are now aware that when depression strikes a man it is not only his problem, but a problem for the significant others in his life as well.

If Your Partner Is Depressed

Annette watched her husband's mood deteriorate:

He stopped washing and shaving and cutting his hair. He'd spend hours staring at the TV screen, even after I had switched the television off. I missed talking to him and sharing my day. Whenever I asked him what was wrong, he'd just tell me he was fine, but I knew he wasn't fine. He stopped talking to me, he didn't eat with me anymore, he didn't even look at me anymore. He used to walk the dog every morning, share the chores and the bills. Now I'm walking the dog, doing all the chores and paying all the bills.

All couple relationships – whether gay or straight, monogamous or open – are characterized by intimacy, both physical and emotional. You express feelings with a partner that you wouldn't with anyone else. Your partner sees your vulnerable side. You have a commitment together. You often share responsibilities together. Your lives are joined in a special way.

When your partner withdraws because of his depression, you will miss the intimacy you once shared. It will feel as if there is a huge gap in your life. The underlying structure of your relationship alters. Roles may change. For example, if you always had an equal relationship, you may now find yourself always being the listener or always doing the chores. You may also find that you have to bear a greater financial burden because your partner is too depressed to work. Routines will change. Your partner may not fulfil his responsibilities or his role within the family: household chores, paying bills, caring for the children, organizing things, etc.

You will have less time to take care of yourself and your other family members and friends. You may even find yourself turning down opportunities or invitations. Linda was offered promotion, but because it involved two evening shifts she declined. She was worried that if she took it, her boyfriend Ray would feel lonely and isolated.

The chances are your partner is not as interested in seeing friends and doing things, so your social life starts to crumble. 'He just seems to have lost his get up and go,' says Judith. 'What I wouldn't give for an evening out.' When he does go out, he may be irritable, sarcastic and moody, and gradually friends may start to avoid seeing the both of you. Making plans to go anywhere won't be easy. At the last minute he may decide that he isn't up to it. 'We never go out anymore' is a common complaint made by partners of depressed men.

Intimacy and sexuality often become non-existent. 'I can't remember the last time we had sex,' says Owen. 'He feels more like my brother than my partner.' Sometimes, though, his emotional neediness becomes suffocating, and you may find his dependency a burden.

There may be a breakdown in communication. Interactions tend to be characterized by miscommunication, misunderstanding, tension and resentment. Stephen, who had been depressed for some time, felt that his wife Margaret was self-centred. Margaret felt angry that he wasn't appreciating her efforts to relate to him. Whenever Stephen spoke about his troubles, she would talk about her own to show her empathy. Both felt misunderstood, and blamed each other for their unhappiness.

You may feel sympathy at first and try to help, but as time goes on you may begin to feel frustrated by the situation. Sue felt great sympathy for her partner Liam when his mother died, but when he continued to be depressed and didn't snap out of it she got annoyed and even angry, wishing that things would go back to normal.

Depression in a loved one may be hard to confront because of your feelings of anger. You may feel that your loved one is trying to punish you or that you are responsible in some way. Mandy felt that her husband was 'getting back' at her for an affair she had had years before.

You may also worry about what others will think. You could be concerned that other people will consider your partner crazy or blame you for his changed behaviour and sadness.

The changes depression brings are likely to put a huge strain on your relationship. They are also likely to make any stressful issues you have in your relationship more pronounced. 'We always used to argue about money, but when he got depressed the issue got blown out of all proportion,' says Laura, whose husband James is seriously depressed.

Research shows that men in relationships are less likely to get depressed, but it also shows that if a relationship is conflicted or difficult, this can deepen a man's depression and threaten the relationship. If ways aren't found to cope with the situation, in many cases the mutual friction, tension and resentment lead to a loss of intimacy and warmth between you which prolongs the depression and shortens the relationship.

If Your Son Is Depressed

Bringing a son into the world is for most parents a source of pride and joy. The task of rearing a son is invested with great hope for the future. Parents look for affirming signs of normality. They worry about his education, his employability, his ability to succeed in the world and have close, loving relationships. It is hard for parents not to feel that they have failed in some way when depression emerges. So much is at stake: not just the future of the son, but the future of the family itself.

You may feel that you are somehow to blame, and be questioning your parenting skills. You will also worry about how your son's depression will affect other children you have, and your relationship. It's all too easy to start blaming yourself and your partner for doing something to trigger the depression. The very fact that this time you can't 'kiss it better,' as you could other childhood woes, will increase your sense that you have been an incompetent parent.

Danny has taken me to hell and back. I've given up my evening classes. I work only part-time. My whole world revolves around him. He is my world and I love him, but at times I feel so frustrated by it all. Where did I go wrong?

Samantha

The belief that childhood should be a time of sunshine and smiles may be deeply ingrained, so that your biggest challenge may be recognizing and accepting that your son is depressed. Remember, symptoms of depression in children are often masked in normal developmental behaviour like tantrums and clingyness in boys or rebellion in teenagers. Your son may manifest typical signs such as sadness and sleep disorders, or he may become aggressive and destructive. Teachers, friends and other family members may notice before you do that he isn't himself or that he isn't enjoying activities or interests like he used to.

Parents always worry about their children, but when depression strikes peace of mind is completely destroyed. Most parents become even more watchful, protective and paranoid. You may find it incredibly hard to keep to your regular routine, and your child will take up much, if not all, of your time. Family life can be totally disrupted. He may resent his dependent position, and you may feel anxious and uncertain about how to provide appropriate care now and in the future.

If your son is no longer a child, your relationship changes somewhat. You don't have the same influence over his behaviour. Your role becomes similar to that of an intimate friend. Most parents find dealing with depression in adult children very hard. You may feel even more confused about how much you should intervene and how much you need to respect his need for autonomy. The sorrow, guilt, anxiety and concern are just as intense, but now you will feel even more powerless because you have less control over his life.

If Your Brother Is Depressed

Having a depressed brother is challenging. You may feel guilty that it was something you said or did. You may feel jealous that he is getting more attention from your parents than you ever did. You may develop your own set of symptoms, or you may feel that you shouldn't complain if you are unhappy, because you don't want to burden your parents any further.

If you are at school or college together, your brother's anti-social behaviour may embarrass you. Whatever your age, you will miss the brother he used to be and the way your family was before he got depressed. You may feel anxious that responsibility for him may fall into your hands if your parents can't take care of him.

You may worry that you will get depressed too, since the tendency runs in the families. It is important that you understand that, although your risk of depression is greater because of genetics and being in close contact with a depressed person, this doesn't mean that you will get depressed too.

If Your Father Is Depressed

Many children with a father who is depressed don't recognize that he is depressed. They mistake his symptoms for physical ailments and behaviours typical of older people. As mentioned earlier, older men are even more unlikely than younger men to seek treatment. You may have a clearer idea of how to identify signs of depression, but the generation gap between you and your father may cloud his judgement. For him, depression may still carry an embarrassing stigma. He may tend to accept his lot stoically. It wouldn't occur to him to seek help.

If your father is depressed, this may have an effect on your self-esteem, especially if he was depressed when you were growing up. Some experts believe that the irritability and emotional absence of depressed fathers may produce children who are more prone to anxiety and depression themselves. According to a Yale University study, the risk of depression, anxiety disorders, hospitalization, poor health and other behavioural problems increases significantly if your father or mother were depressed when you were growing up.

Some children become so carefully attuned to their father's moods that in adult life a compulsive need to please others develops. Many women whose fathers were depressed have little sense of self-worth and fall victim to dysfunctional, abusive relationships.

If your father is depressed you may feel guilty and responsible. Your father may make matters worse by reinforcing these feelings. Amy's father used to explode with rage if her room was untidy. Bob's father would lash out if his university grades weren't good enough. Bob knew the sacrifice his father was making to pay for his education, but however hard he tried he never felt that he could live up to his father's expectations.

You may get very distracted from your own life when your father experiences a depressive mood.

You may take it upon yourself to care for your depressed father. Michael's father moved in with him when his depression was at its most severe. After two years, Michael was broken down and exhausted.

All the time I had to take off work to drive him to hospital appointments. All the clearing up I had to do after him. I didn't have any life. It was the hardest thing I have ever had to do, but I got my father hospitalized. I couldn't cope anymore.

You may find that you have to limit your input for your own survival.

Hopefully you will have other family members to share your concern with, but if you alone feel responsible for your father, the issue of boundaries and autonomy needs to be established. You need to be clear in your own mind how much you are going to get involved in your father's life, and how much you are going to parent him. You need to feel comfortable with the situation. And the chances are that if you are getting involved out of a sense of duty or because you feel guilty, the situation won't be positive for you or for him.

If a Friend Is Depressed

Depression in a male friend can have a big impact on your own mood. How you feel and react can have an effect on your ability to help. If you feel angry, resentful or worried, your friend may respond in a negative way and a vicious cycle establishes itself.

Friendships tend to be less permanent than relationships with partners or family. Because they are more transitory, people may be less willing to expose their vulnerable sides. With less openness, misunderstanding and miscommunication are common.

Christopher is getting increasingly frustrated with his friend David. Every time they arrange to meet, David cancels at the last minute. Christopher suspects that David is depressed, but is nervous about broaching the subject. He is afraid of offending David. David feels pressured by Christopher at the moment, and can't find a way to tell him that he gets anxiety attacks.

The first area of difficulty is when incorrect assumptions are made. Depression in a friend may be attributed to selfishness, as when he doesn't return your calls or seems preoccupied, and you may decide to end the friendship. Even if you do recognize that a friend, colleague or pupil is depressed, the next hurdle is how to deal with the situation without embarrassing him or seeming to interfere. You have no idea what his reaction will be.

This brings us to the central problem: how to talk constructively about feelings without humiliating him. In Part 2 you'll learn how you can express your feelings in a manner that will minimize his defensiveness and optimize his openness, so that collaboration – and not isolation – can be the result. You will also learn how to introduce the subject of depression to a man who doesn't know he is depressed. For the man who uses depression as an excuse to treat you badly, you will see how you can confront the matter in a way that is beneficial to the both of you.

Co-dependent Relationships

I had expected so much of this marriage. I had so many dreams, but none of them came true. I had been tricked and betrayed. My home had become a trap, and I couldn't find a way out. Maybe, I kept telling myself, he will get better. After all, the problems are his fault. When he gets over his depression and sobers up, our marriage will get better.

Most of the time I felt guilty. I sometimes wondered if I am going crazy. Something horrible had happened to me and ruined my life. For six years I had become immersed in his depression, and the ways I had been affected became my problem. It didn't matter whose fault it was anymore. I was out of control.

Jessica, age 30

Most of us won't lose ourselves totally when depression strikes in a man we care about, but perhaps you identify in some way with Jessica's words. All relationships have some elements of co-dependency in them.

Co-dependency forms when one person takes an inappropriate amount of responsibility for another. In the case of depression, there can be a blurring of boundaries between the caregiver and the depressed man, which has a toxic effect on both parties. Co-dependants give until they are angry, exhausted and empty of everything. Sometimes a woman can give and suffer so much that it can drive her to the brink. Lisa died at the age of 33, when chronic stress induced a heart attack. Her husband was an alcoholic, constantly in and out of prison.

Over-responsible caregivers take care of everyone except themselves. They are people-pleasers. They feel they know what a depressed man should do, and they blame themselves when he doesn't do it. They have great empathy and insight into how other people are feeling, but they don't know how they are feeling. They believe that everything rests on his depression.

Once he gets better, everything will be all right and life will work again.

The compassion that a co-dependent person feels for a depressed man has its dangerous and manipulative side. Over-responsible behaviour is self-destructive. It is helping gone too far. By remaining attached to men who are destroying themselves, and by taking care of them, co-dependants learn how to destroy themselves. This habit leads them into destructive relationships that won't work. They feel compelled to help a man with depression, anticipate his needs and take charge of his care. Sometimes so much of their identity is wrapped up in taking care of a depressed man and blaming him for all their troubles that his recovery is not in their best interests.

When depression strikes a man you care about, it is all too easy to over-identify with his pain and make it the centre of your existence. Women are especially vulnerable to this, so ingrained is the notion of woman as nurturer and caregiver. But over-identification with his depression won't help him or you. Maintaining your own identity and boundaries is an essential part of the helping process. What's more, taking too much responsibility robs the depressed man of the most essential ingredient he needs for his own recovery: recognition that he must be actively involved in the process.

If you think that you may have a tendency towards over-identification with someone else's troubles, it is vital that you start recognizing how much his depression is affecting your life. It is natural that you are concerned about him and want to help, but this doesn't mean that his problems are your problems. Recognizing the effect his depression has on you, establishing boundaries and taking care of yourself are essential if your relationship is to stand any chance of surviving this hurdle.

How Much Is He Affecting You?

Most of us won't go to co-dependent extremes, but it's often the case that family and friends of a depressed man are so intent on helping him that they are blind to the ways in which they themselves are being affected. Yet if you can start to reflect on your interactions with him, you will begin to recognize that you have very strong feelings yourself.

A crucial step to take if you want to find a way to help a man who is depressed is to acknowledge how his depression is influencing you. Talking or writing about how his depression is affecting you can help you feel healthier, less burdened down, less anxious, and better able to help him.

Think about your last few interactions, and try to recall, as much as possible, your feelings and reactions. The following questions, taken from the many surveys mental health experts provide for caregivers, will help you do this. Be prepared to accept that many of the feelings you have about him won't be positive, but it is important that you recognize and own your feelings, however negative they may be. Studies show that suppressing emotions can affect your physical and emotional health and can put you at greater risk of cardiac disease, cancer, impaired immune response, stomach upsets, fatigue, stress-related headaches, anxiety and depression.

Questionnaire

- Have you made adjustments to your social and work life so that you can cope with his depression?
- Have you spent more money than you usually do because of his condition? Are you in debt?
- Are you less productive at work?
- Have your routines, like mealtimes and bedtime, changed?

- Do you feel that he has changed since he became depressed?
- What was your initial reaction to his depression? How do you feel about it now?
- Have you modified your behaviour towards him? Do you find it hard to know what to say to him?
- Have you told anyone else about how you are feeling?
- Has his depression caused friction in your relationship with him?
- Do you feel that you have neglected other people and other interests because of his depression?
- Do you feel that you have no control over your life anymore?
- Do you feel weighed down?
- Do you feel lonely?
- Do you feel anxious?
- Do you feel sad?
- Do you worry about the future?
- Do you feel embarrassed to talk about his depression?
- Do you feel that you are somehow to blame?
- Do you resent that you have more responsibilities because of his depression?
- Have people noticed that you have been a bit down lately?
- Do you feel that you aren't helping him enough?
- Do you feel angry and frustrated?
- Do you ever get the urge to run away from the situation?
- Do you find it hard to concentrate on your own life?
- Do you feel hopeless and anxious yourself?

If you find yourself answering 'yes' to most of these questions, this will help you to recognize how great an impact his depression is having on all areas of your life.

Most therapists and doctors agree that is important to both your own well-being and that of the man you care about that you pay attention to how you are feeling. Inattention to your own feelings and reactions affects your health and your ability to help and support him.

For those of you who are natural givers, it won't be easy to focus on yourself rather than the depressed man. However, it will be worth the effort. It will give you the tools you need to cope with the situation.

The next section of the book is designed to show you how to help a depressed man, but it will begin with the first and most important step: helping yourself. This will enable you to cope with the impact his depression is having on your life.

How to Help

Concern should drive us into action,
not into a depression.

Karen Horney

5

How to Help Yourself

It's surprising how many persons go through life without ever recognizing that their feelings toward other people are largely determined by their feelings toward themselves, and if you're not comfortable within yourself you can't be comfortable with others.

Sydney J Harris

I wasn't aware of it at the time, but in photographs taken of me when my boyfriend was depressed I look ill, thin and tired. One photograph in particular stands out. I'm in a park and it's snowing. I'm forcing a smile, even though I look freezing.

The reason I had no warm clothes on is that all my efforts that morning had been focused on getting my boyfriend to take a walk. I had a headache and needed some fresh air. I knew he didn't want to go for a walk, and I knew he didn't want to be left alone. If I stayed in I would feel worse, and if I went out I would worry about him. In the end I managed to pressure him into going with me, but the effort took its toll. I felt I was being selfish. He resented the pressure. And I was so intent on going for the walk that when I realized it was too cold, I didn't want to turn back for fear we wouldn't go out again.

Thinking about what you want when a man you care about is depressed may cause conflict within yourself. You may think of self-care as selfish. He is the one who needs help, not you. But if you don't take care of yourself, how can you possibly have the strength and resilience to cope with the situation?

Self-care

You have probably heard at some time or another the advice that only after you love yourself can you love someone else. The same applies to helping someone else.

Only after you know how to care for yourself can you care for someone else.

Common sense and scientific research agree that, until you meet your own physical and emotional needs, you can't muster sufficient resources to help anyone else. When self-care is ignored for the sake of a depressed man, you simply can't be most effective in helping or taking care of him. In the course of writing this book I spoke to men and women who ignored their basic needs and gave their all to help. In most cases they were the first to acknowledge that their exhaustion undermined their efforts to be an effective helper.

When You Reach Your Limit

Feelings of helplessness, guilt, anger and loneliness, added to the urgency and tension caused by the demands a man's depression places on your own strength, time and energy, may well make you feel that you are overwhelmed. When you feel stretched beyond your ability to cope, when you feel physically and emotionally exhausted, you may experience what Dr Herbert J Freudenberger has termed 'burnout' or compassion fatigue.

Freudenberger's research shows that some positive character traits, such as commitment, dedication, being a giver, and a willingness to work hard and maintain order can all contribute to burnout. It's often the case that the most capable, caring and energetic people find themselves overwhelmed by the responsibilities of caring for another person.

Burnout has dangerous consequences for you and for the depressed man in your life. If you feel you can't cope anymore and need to leave, this will make him feel even more isolated. On the other hand, if you stay you may get seriously depressed yourself and isolate yourself even more from other people.

Should you reach a point when both of you are exhausted and feeling hopeless, it is essential that you involve other people and seek help from friends, family or your doctor. If you don't think you have reached that point yet, you still need to pay attention to the warning signs, and you need to know how to manage the stress of the situation to avoid burnout.

Warning Signs

When burnout occurs, certain physical and emotional reactions are likely. These include headaches, backache, fatigue, stomach upsets, poor resistance to infection and difficulty sleeping.

You may also feel empty, sad, frustrated, resentful, angry, insecure, apathetic, overwhelmed, burdened down and confused. 'I feel like a washing machine that has been too tightly loaded. It is an effort to get around' is how Ann, whose husband suffers from post-traumatic stress disorder, describes her situation.

You may wonder why you are trying to help him, why you are concerned at all, if there is any point to what you are doing. You may be quickly frustrated by minor irritations which you could normally deal with. In retrospect you may realize, as Ann did, that your short fuse is associated with too much responsibility:

I remember flying off the handle for very little reason. Supermarket queues, cashpoints that didn't work, poor customer service were like a red rag to a bull for me. I would explode with anger and outrage.

Avoiding Burnout

Avoiding burnout involves finding the right balance between your needs and those of the depressed man. Don't automatically assume that anything you want is selfish and unfair because he is depressed. He is in a more vulnerable position and needs special consideration, but this does not mean that your needs are not important. Striking a healthy balance is what matters.

The following self-help tips are designed to help you strike that balance and avoid burnout.

1 Understand Depression

Knowledge is power. Not knowing what you are dealing with can make you feel helpless and confused.

Part 1 of this book was devoted to understanding male depression, to bring clarity to a much-misunderstood and neglected subject. Later in this book we will discuss suggested treatments. The information given has been kept intentionally brief, so that you don't get too bogged down, distracted and overwhelmed. But should you want to know more, the suggested reading list at the back of the book will give you additional and more detailed information.

It can be hard to determine if a man is depressed, because men tend to be uncommunicative and to withdraw when they are troubled. Chapter 2 outlined how you can recognize the symptoms of depression if you aren't sure. In Chapter 6 we'll explore in more detail the helpful and unhelpful ways to approach a man when he is under stress, and how to cope when he turns your help away.

2 Understand How Men Process Feelings

A basic understanding of male psychology and male tendencies can help prevent misunderstandings and miscommunication. Men and women often badly mislead each other when they talk out of different perspectives, agendas and interests.

Listed below are some internal processing methods often favoured by males, according to Michael Gurian, therapist and author of *The Wonder of Boys* and *A Fine Young Man*. Bear in mind, though, that each man is an individual and the following is only a generalization. Nevertheless, hopefully it will help you make better sense of things when he insists he is 'fine', but you are not so sure.

1   The action-release method
    Men often process and release feelings through action. They may
    angrily yell at you, fly off the handle, slam a door, hit the table or
    just turn off by burying themselves in some activity like reading
    the newspaper. This may seem like rejection to you, but it isn't.
    It is simply a way of processing feelings that may be different
    from yours.

2   Delayed-reaction method
    Many women notice that their men deal with emotional problems
    in a delayed-reaction way. It's common for a man to wait weeks
    until he tells anyone about what is worrying him, while in the
    meantime he may seem irritable or distant with you. You may
    wonder if you have done something wrong. More often than
    not, you haven't.

3   Objectification method
    Women notice that the men they love tend to make objects of
    emotions. They may displace their emotions onto other things or

people – for instance, on the success or failure of their favourite football team. You may find this cold and distancing.

4   Physical expression method

Men tend to experience, express and expel their feelings physically to a greater degree than women. Sport, for example, can be a great stress-reliever. You may feel neglected if your partner is constantly running off to the gym, but he is probably giving himself an avenue for emotional expression.

5   Withdrawal method

A man may feel overwhelmed when emotions swirl upon him or when feelings are verbalized. He may need time away on his own, in another part of the house. You may think he is trying to get away from you, but it's not you he is escaping from. He is trying to get away from stimulation so that he can process information.

6   Problem-solving method

Solving problems releases emotional energy for many men and they quickly feel better. You may feel that he has not invested as much emotional energy as you think he should, but this may simply be his way of working. Addressing a problem that agitates a man can help relieve his stress.

The internal processing methods that tend to be least favoured by men are talking and crying.

Crying may be a terrifying experience for a man. His brain is processing emotive data in a fast and confusing way, and he may feel he is losing himself. He has been taught that men don't cry, and this only adds to his confusion and feelings of vulnerability.

This doesn't mean a man can't talk or cry about how he feels, it just means that talking and crying about feelings don't come as naturally to him as to a woman. For a man to express how he feels, he needs to feel that he is in a safe and supportive environment, and the timing has to be right.

The suggested reading list at the end of this book includes materials on male psychology, and you might want to research this further. In the next chapter we'll look at how a basic understanding of male psychology can help you encourage a man who seems unhappy or depressed to talk about his feelings in a way that won't alienate or humiliate him.

3 Teamwork

The third self-help tip for avoiding burnout is to give yourself time to consider how your needs can be constructively met within the confines of the relationship. Try as much as you can to convey to the depressed man in your life the sense that you are a team. His and your needs are equally important. That way, neither of you will assume that the answer lies in isolation.

Involve him in your dilemma if you can, but don't make him feel responsible for it. If something concerns you, tell him that you aren't sure what to do but you would appreciate his input. If at all possible, look for ways that he can help you. For instance, if you want to go out, and you make a point of thanking him for making the effort to come with you because you understand it is difficult for him, he may feel less like a burden.

4 Meet Your Own Deeper Needs

Everyone in the world has three basic emotional needs: We need to feel valued, respected, or loved by others; we need to feel in control of our lives; we need to know we are getting things right. When a man gets depressed, you may find that all your deeper needs are threatened. He tells you he doesn't care anymore; you don't feel in control of your life; the more he suffers, the less value you place on your helping skills.

As hard as it may seem, it is crucial that you don't put your own life on hold and that you continue to get your basic needs met. If you don't, you will end up in pain. To help the man you care about, you need to feel energized. Everyone needs time to feel productive and to nourish themselves and their interests.

Remember, you are a separate person. Even though he is suffering, keep your life going; maintain your friendships. You may be feeling miserable, but continue activities that give you pleasure, or take up new interests, even though it may be hard for you to think about anything else.

You can't give all the time. Don't make the mistake of giving up your life and thinking that everything you do outside of his depression is worthless.

5 Keep Your Daily Routines

When life seems to be out of control, one of the most effective ways to regain control is to have daily routines that give you a sense of structure and safety.

It's impossible ever to fully control your life, but it can be comforting to keep up routines that are familiar to you. For instance, getting up at the same time, having dinner at the same time, working or attending the gym can help you feel that your own life continues to have structure. Depression is such an unpredictable illness; maintaining familiar routines can remind you that there is still an element of order in your life.

6 Watch Your Physical Health

You can't help him if you are exhausted, ill and lacking energy yourself. It really isn't selfish to take care of your own physical health. Make sure you eat well and get enough sleep, daylight and regular exercise. A workout can be a great tension-releaser, too. Avoid smoking, alcohol and drugs, and keep your weight steady. If you have any physical ailments, see a doctor.

7 Get a Sense of Perspective

Many of the caregivers I spoke to said that the world seems to vanish when you care for a depressed man. Depression can be all-consuming. You may find that days and weeks go by when you aren't aware of what is going on in the world around you. You are not even sure what day of the month it is. Everything revolves around him and his needs.

Try to remember that life doesn't stop just because the man you care about is depressed.

Every person's life involves certain difficulties and pains. It can be comforting to remind yourself of this. Take an interest in the news, other people, and what is going on around you to keep a sense of perspective.

You may find that simply sitting in a park and watching people go by is reassuring. Or you may find that the awesome beauty of nature gives you a sense of calm – the stillness of dawn, the beauty of the night sky, the passing of the seasons. Take advantage of anything that reminds you that life goes on and that, even though his suffering seems of monumental importance to you and him, it has a tiny place in the general scheme of things.

8 Set Yourself Free

Control is an illusion. It doesn't work. You cannot control any man's moods. A depressed man will ultimately do what he wants to do, think what he wants to think, and feel what he wants to feel. It doesn't matter that you could help him if only he'd do this or that. It doesn't matter.

You can't change people. This is hard to accept, especially if a man you care about is hurting himself, but that's the way it is.

Letting go of your need to control doesn't mean you don't care. In fact, it shows how much you do care. The greatest love of all is the love that gives a man freedom to choose. It can be frightening to detach yourself in this way, but, as we'll explain in Chapter 6, it is the only way forward.

9 Involve Others

Letting go also makes you more receptive to the help and concern of others. Your instinct may be to try and shut others out, but time and time again studies have shown that sharing your problem with people you trust eases the burden and stops you feeling so isolated.

Allow yourself to be replenished by others. Accept help if you need it. Ask for help if you need it. You can't do everything. Talking to other people in the same position as you can be especially helpful. You won't feel so isolated and stigmatized, and you may get some useful coping techniques. Talk to your doctor, or contact a group such as MIND in the UK or DART in the US for information about support groups in your area.

Professional counsellors take at least an hour a week with other counsellors to off-load the pain passed to them by clients. Consider what emotional support you are getting or can get from friends and family or your partner. If the answer is none, ring a support group. They can help you consider your options and replenish your energy.

10 Be Open and Honest

You may well find that his depression calls upon you to make excuses for him. If you are invited to social functions together and he doesn't want to attend, you may say that he 'has to work late' or that he has a 'stomach upset' or 'a bout of flu'. When you do this you are, in effect, becoming his enabler.

An enabler is someone who makes it possible for a man to continue with his depression without it being detected by others. Few if any caregivers could say that they have never told falsehoods or white lies to hide the truth. Each time Janet phoned work for her husband to say that he had a cold or the flu or a back injury, she felt 'nervous and uncomfortable. I hate telling lies.'

As an enabler, without realizing it you may also be protecting yourself from the emotional pain of his condition. It's easier and more comfortable for you to hide the truth from others. The danger is that hiding the truth from others comes close to denial:

I got so used to lying for Ralph, making excuses and covering up his mistakes, that it became second nature. In my mind he wasn't really depressed, he was just a little down. I wanted to believe he was OK.

Rebecca

As hard as it is, a better response would be to find a way to tell the truth without humiliating the depressed man. Stigma about depression in men abounds, so don't expect this to be easy.

The situation gets even more complicated when the man you care about wants you to cover up for him, and asks you to lie or make excuses. Collaborating with him may seem like the best option in the short term, but in the long term it only makes the problem worse. You may find that telling others creates problems for him and for you, but if keeping secrets makes you feel uncomfortable, tell him that you both need to find another way to deal with the situation.

You may find that you need to involve another person or your doctor or a counsellor if you can't agree on a resolution.

11 Stop Blaming Yourself

Joanne never wanted to have children, and made that clear when she married Noel, but when Noel was diagnosed with depression, Joanne blamed herself. 'If we'd had children, maybe he wouldn't have got depressed.'

Joanne felt directly responsible for her husband's depression. You may feel responsible for his moods in a less direct way. Misery loves company, and you may find yourself slowing your own progress and blaming yourself for his moods.

At the height of my boyfriend's depression I started to think it was all my fault. We both worked in the same field, and his decline began when my career really took off. In some bizarre way, I felt that my success was making it harder for him to cope. Looking back, I wonder how on earth I could have come to that conclusion, but many of you with depressed men will relate to this kind of self-blame and distorted thinking.

It is important to remember that each of us makes life choices, but these life choices can't make a man depressed. At the time, the decisions you made were the ones that you thought were best. You have no control over the effects of those life choices and how the man you care about chooses to react to them.

You are also not to blame if the man chooses to cope with his depression by withdrawing. Try to understand that his withdrawal and sadness have nothing to do with you and everything to do with the fact that he is depressed. It's been said earlier, but it's important to mention this again: You can't make a man depressed by what you say, do, or feel. *His depression is not your fault.*

12 Take Time to Relax

Relaxation is the time when you recharge your batteries and focus on what makes you feel good. Unfortunately, many caregivers tend to neglect setting aside time and space for themselves. Many find it impossible to relax at all.

If you can't relax, you need to learn how to take time out. One way to do this is to relax your whole body slowly, muscle by muscle. There are many tapes on the market that can help you through the process. You could also try counting to 10 before you react, or repeat some positive affirmation to yourself like, 'I am in control.'

Deep, slow breathing through the nose rather than the mouth, allowing your abdomen to move, can calm both body and mind and help you cope with stress. Simple yoga breathing exercises, for example breathing in slowly through the nose while counting to five in your head, holding your breath for a count of five, breathing out slowly through the nose for a count of five, waiting a count of five and repeating as often as you like, may also help. Concentrating on breathing and counting can be wonderfully calming for your mind, while the regular breathing will calm the body.

There are many helpful ways to relax. Soothing music, soaking in a hot tub, laughing more, interacting with others, having a positive outlook, cultivating outside interests, and diversions from your routine can all help. You should not think of these activities as time lost, but as time gained. When you return to your daily routine, you should feel refreshed, energized and in control, with a better perspective on things.

You Can Do Only So Much

Making use of these suggestions may help you feel less exhausted and burdened, but if they don't, this is a clear sign that you need help from friends, family, your doctor or a support group. You need to recognize that you can't cope anymore by yourself. You need to recognize that there is only so much you can do.

Caregivers often feel that there must be something more they can do, something they can say that will ease the situation. 'If I just take my son to America for a three-week vacation, I'm sure he will get over it,' says Matthew. 'If I could just earn more money, then he wouldn't have to work so hard,' says Lorna. 'If I could just make sure that we spend more time together,' says Bridget. When a man you care about is depressed, there is always something more you think you can do and there are always more responsibilities you think you should take on. You will probably feel that you have never done enough.

How much should you get involved? How much responsibility should you take? What should you do for him? What should you expect him to do for himself? Much depends on the nature of your relationship, but much also depends on whether you can recognize if you are overwhelmed or not.

If you over-involve yourself in his depression, if you monitor his every move, if you eagerly watch for every sign that his depression may return, if you start treating him like a child who can't cope without you, if the boundaries between you start to blur, if your own health is suffering, then the situation between you has got out of control and is unproductive and unhealthy for the both of you. You may even be enabling his depression. Unconsciously, you may be behaving in a way that makes it possible for him to continue with his depression or allow it to go untreated.

To be an effective support for a depressed man, you need to recognize that there is only so much you can do. You also need to be able to take care of yourself.

Caring for Him

If you want to care for a depressed man, taking care of yourself and having a healthy sense of self are essential. When you have a healthy sense of self, you can reach out to others for help. You can let go of your need to control him, and trust in his ability to cope. You can support him because you are strong enough physically and emotionally to cope with all the uncertainties. You can *care for* him rather than *take care* of him.

When you *take care* of a depressed man, you may assume responsibilities for his needs and feelings. You take control and expect him to do things your way. You neglect your own needs, lose a sense of your own boundaries, and often feel tired, burdened and resentful because so much of your personal energy is tied up in his welfare. You're not helping him, and you're certainly not helping yourself.

When you *care for* a depressed man, you do not do for him what he can and should do for himself. You do not assume responsibility for his emotional state. You do not make demands of him or expect him to behave in a certain way. You do not control. You consider meeting your own needs as important as meeting his. You retain a sense of boundaries. It is possible for you to feel relaxed and free despite the pressures that are upon you. You are able to be a help and support to him without losing control over your own life.

The most effective ways to go about caring for, helping and supporting a man when he is depressed will be discussed in the chapters that follow.

6

Helping Him

Mary: What's wrong, Michael?
Silence.
Mary: I can tell something is wrong.
Silence.
Mary: For God's sake, talk to me.
Silence.
Mary: Tell me what's wrong.
Michael: Nobody cares.
Mary: That's ridiculous. How can you say that? I care about you.
Michael: You don't understand.
Mary: Understand what?
Silence.
Mary: Is it something I have done?
Silence.
Mary: Why won't you talk to me?
Michael: Things aren't great at work.
Mary: Oh, Michael, that's rough. I know how you feel. Thing's aren't great with my job either, but look, I'm coping, and so can you.
Michael: What's the point?
Mary: Don't let it get to you, Michael.
Silence.
Mary: You'll be fine.
Silence.
Michael: It's not just work. It's everything.
Mary: Everything is going to work out fine, you'll see.

Mary: Don't walk away, Michael. Where are you going?
The door slams shut.
Mary spends the rest of the day feeling anxious, worried, guilty and responsible.

Like Mary, you may find yourself responding to the worries and fears of the man you care about with frustration, denial and defensiveness. It's hardly surprising, when you consider how unsettling his behaviour is and how much he is hurting you.

In the brief fictional dialogue above, Mary made some very common mistakes. She approached the situation with the best of intentions, but the dialogue was fraught with tension and misunderstanding. In this chapter you'll learn what these common mistakes are, and why efforts to reach out so often end up being counterproductive.

You'll also learn that there are better ways to approach a man and encourage him to talk when he seems depressed.

You may find that improved communication involves approaching the situation in a totally new way. Don't expect this to be easy, and give yourself plenty of time to adapt. Your ability to comfort a depressed man may depend on the following essential steps, some of which may be unfamiliar to you:

1   Recognizing if you are the person to help
2   Recognizing if he actually needs your help
3   Encouraging him to talk
4   Setting boundaries
5   Helping him acknowledge how he feels
6   Bringing focus to the dialogue

Let's explore each of these in turn.

1 Recognizing If You Are the Person to Help

You want to help the man in your life who is depressed, but are you the right person to give that help?

Think about your motivations. Are you lonely? Do you want gratitude? Do you feel you ought to help, but secretly feel resentful? Do you have another agenda for helping him?

Do you have too many other responsibilities which have to take priority in your life? Young children, for example, or a medical condition that makes it unwise to take on extra stresses? Or are you just too emotionally involved?

When Christopher's son threatened suicide, Christopher knew that he wasn't the one to help. He was too scared, angry and frightened. He was falling to pieces. The thought of losing his son was too terrifying for him to contemplate. In the end, counsellors and the support of family and friends pulled him through the crisis.

If you think you are not the right person to do the job of helping, understand that you are helping him more by stepping aside or letting him know what your priorities are. It isn't your fault that you are not the person, so stop feeling guilty. Let someone else do the job.

The idea of helping can seem very appealing, and in many cases helping others is very rewarding. But the opposite can be true, too. Sometimes supporting another person can be disappointing, frustrating and difficult. You feel unappreciated and uncomfortable. You may even wonder why you bothered in the first place. We've discussed burnout in the last chapter, but here are other common problems helpers can face and which you need to be aware of:

HE TURNS AGAINST YOU

At the beginning he welcomes or even invites your help, and you give as much as you can with the best of intentions, but then he or one of his family or friends decides you are the wrong person to help him. He or they may even start to see you as the cause of his problems. If you have done the best that you can, the chances are that you have become the scapegoat and don't deserve the criticism. Try to resolve the situation, but if this isn't possible you need to be the kind of person who won't take things personally and can step aside to let others help him.

HE DEPENDS ON YOU TOTALLY

When a man depends on you totally, it can cause you considerable anxiety. Once again you started out with the best of intentions, but now he seems incapable of doing anything without you. A part of you worries that this isn't good for him. A part of you feels burdened. Full recovery can occur only when a man takes charge of his own life. If you find him becoming too dependent on you, you need to be able to turn the tables back on him in a gentle way. Ask him what *he* feels is right, what *he* thinks he should do.

HE DOESN'T GET ANY BETTER

You try everything, and he seems to be getting worse, not better. Sometimes he takes a step forwards, but the next week he takes two steps back again. You wonder where you are going wrong, what you can possibly do to make him get better.
  If this is the case, you need to be able to recognize that unfortunately there is little you *can* do; you can't solve his problems for him. He is the one who needs to find a solution; all you can do is offer support and encouragement. If you think he isn't making any effort and this is making you angry, then

perhaps you should consider letting someone else do the supporting.

HE DOESN'T WANT ANYTHING TO DO WITH YOU

Later we'll explore how to cope when a man rejects your help or pushes you away when he is depressed, but you need to be prepared for the possibility that he might reject you once he gets better, too. Despite all your caring and support during the crisis, and despite the fact that the crisis seems to be behind him, he starts to avoid contact with you. He's embarrassed and uncomfortable around you.

Should the man you care about start to reject you, you need to be able to accept the fact that just because you have helped him doesn't automatically mean he is going to be a friend for life. He may become uncomfortable with you because you remind him of an unpleasant time of his life and you are too familiar with his vulnerabilities. Don't let this stop you helping him or other people, but remember that sometimes the price you pay for helping a man who is depressed is losing him.

2 Recognizing If He Actually Needs Your Help

If you think you are the one to help, knowing *when* your help is actually needed is important.

It can often be hard to know if a man is depressed because he won't tell you what is worrying him. The task is made even harder by the fact that the two of you are different people and may want and mean different things. Small clashes of perspective often lie behind many misunderstandings, and this is never more true than when a man is depressed.

If the man in your life copes with crisis by withdrawing into aloneness to simply stare out of the window, allow him these experiences. Try not to take his withdrawal personally. In time he will emerge and be available to you again. It's simply his way of coping with a difficult situation.

If he withdraws because he really doesn't want or need your interference, then jumping in with unwanted advice, help that isn't needed and intimacy that isn't wanted is likely to make the situation worse. If you try to force him to talk before he is ready, it may provoke negative reactions and tension in your relationship. He may become irritable, moody and critical of you. He may react passively with loss of libido, fatigue, or withholding love and affection.

On the other hand, his withdrawal may signal that he really does need your help. You need to be able to spot the difference. If his withdrawal is prolonged (over more than a few weeks) and accompanied by many of the telltale signs of depression outlined in Chapter 2, the chances are that the man you care about is depressed. Even though he is unlikely to request it, he urgently needs your understanding and emotional support.

3 Encouraging Him to Talk

If the man in your life copes with distress by taking time and space to mull things over, he may simply be assuming responsibility for his mistakes. If you are concerned that something is deeply wrong, however, there are ways you can encourage him to discuss his feelings.

You may find that approaching the situation in a way that takes into account how men tend to process feelings is more fruitful than simply asking him to talk about how he feels.

The following guidelines may prove helpful:

DON'T FORCE THE ISSUE

Many men cannot talk readily about what is upsetting them. Don't push the man you know into talking. The best thing to do when reactions are delayed is to be patient, let him know you are there, and remind him that your support always exists for him.

You might ask once if he is OK, wait a few moments, then let it go, letting him come to you in his time. A man who is constantly asked how he feels may, for a while, feel cared for, but if you keep prodding him to talk about his feelings the effect may be to make him defensive and resentful, and to suppress his feelings more. You may be trying to make a man feel better, but if he hasn't asked for your help, he may find it irritating to be questioned about how he is feeling all the time.

The active listening skills described later will let a man know you support him. They will also encourage him to open up to you in his own time.

SPOT BARRIERS IN COMMUNICATION

Common barriers to good communication prevent many men from opening up. Most of these barriers are based on fear of one sort or another: fear of intimacy, fear of rejection, fear of looking silly or of growing apart. It can be difficult to overcome them.

Here are a few of the most common barriers, and suggestions for how to deal with them.

If he is scared of revealing his true feelings because it makes him feel vulnerable –
– Remind him that your relationship can only improve, since love is about trusting someone enough to make ourselves vulnerable.
If he always sidesteps or evades emotional issues –
– Help him understand that, until you know the problem, you can't know how to help him.

If a man feels that emotions are embarrassing or a sign of weakness or insecurity –
– Gently assure him that it's OK to feel: feeling the full range of emotions is part of being a well-rounded, mature adult.
If the man you care about doesn't seem to listen to you or notice your reactions –
– Try to let him know that he can help you feel less frustrated if he allows you to participate fully in communication.

BE SENSITIVE TO THE MAN'S SENSE OF SELF

Since men are socialized to be independent, most aren't going to be comfortable asking for help just because they are depressed. Respect your man's need for independence and don't continually discuss how he is feeling. Most important, don't try to control or baby him, even if you are his mother. You could tell him that you know it's hard for him to be feeling like this, and if there is anything you can do, to let you know. This gives him the power to decide if he needs help or not.

GIVE HIM PLENTY OF SCOPE

It may not be easy for him to talk about his feelings, so give him lots of options. Offer lots of choices for describing how he feels. Don't ask him if he is feeling sad; ask him if he is feeling sad, angry, frightened or worried. Most men will be able to pick out one of the options and start talking. Provide lots of opportunity, and he may decide to share his feelings with you.

WATCH HIS REACTIONS

If you share your experiences with him, pay attention to how he reacts. If the focus changes to you, he may feel competitive. If you equate your feelings with his, he may feel you are not paying attention to his unique circumstances and will express irritation. If he shows defensiveness in any of these ways, it may be a signal that the conversation is not helpful to him. Watch his reactions and be sensitive to them.

BE STRAIGHTFORWARD

When you are presenting information to him, be logical and straightforward. This is no time for hidden agendas or subtle undertones. Simple facts are more helpful than hypothesis and possibilities.

ENCOURAGE HIM TO PROBLEM-SOLVE

If the man you know is fond of a problem-solving approach, encourage him in what works best for him. It will also help if you perfect your own skills in these methods.

He may be used to the language of setting goals. If so, talk about how he can reach his goals. This doesn't mean you solve his problems; it means that, after trying to understand his experience, you ask him about his own ideas for solving his problems. You can also offer, as options to consider, your own suggestions.

ALLOW HIM TO OBJECTIFY HIS EXPERIENCE

This often works much better than the 'What's wrong? Tell me' method. Some men need to connect their feelings to objects in the outside world. For example, let's say you are talking to a man who won't talk to you about what is worrying him. You happen to notice that the football team he supports has been defeated. You could say 'The team must feel very disappointed after all that hard work and anticipation. I bet you feel disappointed like that sometimes, too.'

According to **John Gray** of *Men Are from Mars, Women Are from Venus* fame, one of the most valuable responses you can make to a man under stress is 'What happened?' This helps him to centre himself and become more objective. Then ask him *why* he thinks it happened. Don't ask question after question, though, if he is slow to open up.

LET HIM TAKE ACTION

Give him plenty of opportunity to release his frustration through action that isn't harmful to anyone. This could be an action plan designed to resolve his dilemma. For instance, if his job is causing him stress, he may want to apply for other jobs. Or he could take action in the form of exercise, sport, gardening, odd jobs around the house or hitting a punch bag in the basement.

TIMING IS EVERYTHING

It's true that many men find it difficult to talk about how they feel, but don't let that stop you trying. Try to pick the right moments to ask him how he feels. Timing is everything. You need to approach him when he isn't rushed or stressed and when there are a minimum of distractions. Remember, many men often prefer to focus on one thing at a time. Don't try to launch into a meaningful discussion, for example, when he is watching television or when he is rushing to get to work. Wait until there are no distractions and the two of you are sitting quietly somewhere.

Don't even try to talk until he is in a place where he feels emotionally safe. Until he feels that he can trust you, he is unlikely to open up to you. He needs to feel that you accept him and support him and are not trying to criticize, control or change him. The suggestions in this chapter are all designed to help you establish that atmosphere of acceptance and trust.

4 Setting Boundaries

Giving emotional support to a man when he is depressed can be a full-time job. You need to put limits on when and how long you are going to be there for him. If you don't, things can go horribly wrong. You'll end up like Sam, with no time for yourself or your own life:

When Sam's friend Vincent lost his wife in a car crash, Sam was genuinely upset for him. He helped Vincent with the funeral arrangements and suggested that Vincent ring him at any time.

In the first few weeks, Sam didn't mind that Vincent took him at his word and called him most days. Vincent had had a tough blow and he needed to know that other people cared. The trouble began in the third month, when Vincent started to call in the early hours of the morning. Sam listened and listened, but in the end he switched his answering machine on. Vincent started to call in the evening instead. The answering machine went on again. Vincent left a message on the answering machine accusing Sam of avoiding him. At that point, Sam lost his temper. He called Vincent and told him that he had been as supportive as he could, but that he couldn't help anymore. It was time to move on.

It's easy to drift into supporting someone without thinking through the implications. So the next time you find yourself offering unconditional support, remember that a depressed man may take you at your word. It is much better to set limits and understand what your role is in his crisis from the start, to avoid misunderstandings and tension later on.

When a man is depressed, he often feels that life is out of control. Setting reasonable limits will help create a feeling of safety. He knows where he stands. Be clear with him about what your limits are. Set these limits together if you can. Let him know what you will and won't tolerate. Don't erode the time you take for yourself, and don't let the situation develop to a point when you dread his phone calls or any contact with him. Let him know when you are available and when you are not. If you find it distracting to take calls at work, tell him. If daily contact is too much for you and you would rather see him once a week, make that clear.

You are not a trained counsellor or psychiatrist, so don't set out to be one. You can't solve his problems. You can only listen to them and support him during the crisis.

You can't give everything to him, even if you are his mother or father. You have your own life and your own responsibilities. You can't meet his every emotional need. He will never recover if he doesn't learn to meet his own emotional needs. You will never be able to help him effectively if you don't learn the three golden rules of helping:

1   Do only what he asks of you.
2   Do only what will help him cope better.
3   Do only what you know you can do happily, willingly and well.

You may feel that you are letting him down if you set limits, hold back or simply say no, but taking responsibility for his problems isn't helpful to him. It just means he takes over your life and you feel out of control and resentful. Not giving everything does not mean you are not helping. If you are too exhausted to give anything, you won't be able to help him at all.

Detachment

Learning the art of detachment will help you set limits. Detachment is a technique based on the premise that each person is responsible for himself or herself, that we can't solve problems that aren't ours to solve, and that worry is unproductive. Detachment involves letting go of the need to control, and accepting reality. Detachment means that you learn to love and care and be involved without a blurring of the boundaries between his life and yours. This can be very hard to achieve if you have an intimate relationship.

Detachment doesn't mean you don't care; it simply means that you mentally disengage yourself from unhealthy entanglements with a man's life and with problems you cannot solve. You don't respond to events or their literal context; you respond to the feelings behind them.

For instance, when Michael, in the dialogue that opened this chapter, complained that nobody really cared or understood, Mary quite naturally reminded him of her concern. But by answering in this way she was not addressing Michael's real fear of being abandoned. He feared that he was becoming worthless and that ultimately everyone, including Mary, would reject him when he was at his most needy.

Mary then tried to ask if it was anything she had done. All this does is shift the focus of the discussion. Rather than addressing his pain and confusion, the conversation shifted to the quality of her caring. She felt hurt, angry, and unappreciated by his seeming ingratitude or criticism. He remained as isolated in his pain as ever.

The purpose of detachment is to avoid personalizing what the man you care about is saying or doing, so that you are less likely to be drawn into an argument that neither of you really understands. When you detach you are able to recognize what he is feeling without taking it personally. You are able to look at and to listen to him without responding immediately or bringing the focus of the conversation back to you. Even if he starts criticizing or blaming you or telling you you don't care, you understand that this is not about you, it is about how he feels.

5 Helping Him Acknowledge How He Feels

It is a man's emotions, rather than his thoughts, actions or behaviour, that make him feel most vulnerable. If a depressed man can talk about his emotions or acknowledge how he feels, he will find that he feels relieved. Emotions that aren't expressed can create tension and can actually prevent him from moving on.

When you invite a man to open up to you in an atmosphere of trust, support and without being judgemental, you signal to him that it is OK to feel. That there is no such thing as a 'bad' feeling and that he can feel the full range of emotions available to him, even if those emotions are painful ones.

In your role as helper, you need to let him know that talking about feelings isn't mad, bad or sad. You can do this by using active listening skills like acceptance, keeping silent and mirroring so that he doesn't feel threatened or embarrassed about discussing emotional worries.

Active Listening Skills

ACCEPTANCE

You were probably taught that a caring person gives sympathy to those who are troubled. But that's the last thing a depressed man needs right now. He's feeling bad enough about himself already. He doesn't want you to feel sorry for him as well. Empathy is not sympathy, but acceptance. What he needs is to be listened to without prejudice. What he needs is to feel accepted.

Try to accept what he is feeling. Forget the criticism, the reassurance, being judgemental or dragging out the 'You should pull yourself together' attitude, and accept that he is doing the best that he can to survive. Let him know that you accept him and value him as he is.

For instance, if a man tells you he feels worthless, don't sideline him by telling him you have felt like that too. Don't criticize him, don't feel sorry for him. Don't tell him that he is talking rubbish. Don't tell him that things will be better soon. Don't tell him anything. Instead, ask him to tell you why he feels that way; tell him it's not his fault he feels that way. Let him know that it's OK to have negative feelings, and that you don't think any less of him. He will feel supported and, hopefully, better able to cope.

You may find it hard to accept what a man is saying when you think he doesn't make sense or he is wrong, but acceptance doesn't mean you agree; it just means you accept. Telling a man he is wrong makes him feel defensive, as if he has to justify himself to you. If you simply accept how he feels, he can focus on what is really important – feeling better. Rather than telling him he is wrong, tell him you respect his opinion but that you don't agree.

Not offering advice if you want to help someone is difficult. But when a man is depressed, he doesn't want you to sort out his problems for him. What he needs is time to think things through and to sort out the problem himself. Not judging or criticizing is hard, too. Trained counsellors never judge a person's actions, but if you know you can not be impartial or you think that what he is doing is legally or morally wrong, you need to act as you feel best. Let him know that you can't be impartial, and that if you think it is appropriate you will involve the police or a doctor.

Acceptance takes a lot of practice. Don't get impatient with yourself if you don't always manage it. It's easy to slip back into rejecting, criticizing, advising or passing judgement, but if you keep practising it will get easier. Remember, you don't need to agree with how a man is feeling, you just need to accept and acknowledge it so that he can move on.

KEEPING SILENT

An important part of listening, really listening, to what the man you care about has to say is saying nothing at all. Keeping silent and not reaching out, talking, helping or advising is much harder than it sounds, but acknowledging his pain and not reacting in the moment is an essential part of making him feel accepted.

Your heart may ache when he seems filled with sadness, despair or rage and destructiveness, but trying to engage in conversation in these tension-filled moments will be totally unproductive. Appealing to his reason or for an explanation is futile. If he takes offence at your silence, simply tell him that you want to listen to him and will share your feelings with him later.

Keeping silent is painful, but the pain of that silence is at the heart of the challenge of dealing with a depressed man. You care deeply about him and want to take his pain away. You want to say something to make him feel better. But by demanding that he gets better, as Mary did earlier with Michael, you help yourself and not him.

Unable to deal with the intensity of Michael's emotions, Mary wouldn't accept that Michael was feeling depressed. She bombarded him with statements like 'You can cope,' 'I understand 'cause I've been there,' and 'Everything will work itself out in the end.' From Michael's viewpoint these statements were distancing, patronizing and critical.

Just for a while, you need to put your feelings to one side and focus on what he is feeling. If he senses that you are uncomfortable in any way, you send him the message that feeling hurt is wrong. He puts his feelings on hold, but if feelings are put on hold they became dangerous. If a man can't acknowledge his emotions, he can't move out of his depression.

If you can learn the wisdom of silence, not only do you allow the man you care about to feel heard, you achieve a small victory for yourself as well. You learn that his depression doesn't

control what you say, do or feel. You don't have to react
instantly to what he is saying when he is depressed.

Of course, this doesn't apply when there is an emergency
or you think his life is in danger. I'm not talking about life-
threatening situations here (see Chapter 9). I'm talking about
the typical disagreements that happen on a daily basis between
you and the man who is depressed.

MIRRORING

Another technique to make him see you as a person to whom it
is safe to open up is *mirroring*, or reflecting his feelings. By
using reflection you reinforce his expression of feelings.
Paraphrasing or repeating back what he is saying helps you
convey to him that you are listening and trying to understand.
It also helps you check your own perceptions, to make sure that
you really do understand what he is describing.

For instance, if a man tells you he is tired, under normal circumstances you might suggest that he go and lie down, but this
wouldn't convey to him that he feels understood. A better reply
would be, 'You do sound really exhausted.' If a man tells you
nobody cares about him, rather than saying *you* care, tell him,
'I know it feels that way to you right now.' If a man says he
feels pressured at work because his boss is giving him too much
responsibility, repeat that back to him. 'You feel under pressure
because your boss is giving you too much to do.'

It can be reassuring for a depressed man to feel that you
accept how he feels and are not rejecting him. It's often good to
follow the validation with a supporting statement that can
reassure him that, despite his negative feelings, you will stand
by him. This not only reminds him that you are not going to
abandon him, it also reminds him that feelings change. He feels
like this now, but he won't feel like this for ever. You can offer
him not just validation and reassurance, but hope, too.

AVOIDING VERBAL ROADBLOCKS

To be an effective listener you should avoid statements that shut down the flow of conversation and erode the flow of trust developing between you. Remember that when a depressed man complains, his emotional pain is speaking. Avoid taking what he says literally. Try not to let the verbalization of his pain touch a raw nerve in you so that communication breaks down totally.

Here are some of the most common roadblocks to active listening:

1   Directing, ordering and commanding: 'You must ... You have to ... You will ...'
    Such responses invite defensive communication, hostility or resentment.
2   Warning, threatening, admonishing: 'You had better ... If you don't, then ...'
    This is similar to directing, but this time the element of threat is added.
3   Moralizing, preaching, obliging: 'You should ... You ought ... It's your duty ... responsibility ...'
    This time you drag in duty and some vague external authority. Their purpose is to make him feel guilty or to feel an obligation. Men in trouble sense the pressure of such messages and frequently resist and dig in their heels. Such messages also communicate a lack of trust, as if you're saying he is not wise enough to make his own decisions.
4   Persuading with logic, arguing, instructing, lecturing: 'Do you realize...? ... Here is why you are wrong ... That is not right ... The facts are ... Yes, but ...'
    Such responses provoke defensiveness and often bring on counter-arguments. They may also make the man feel inferior because they imply your superiority. Persuasion, more often than not, simply makes a man defend his position more strongly. Having logic on your side does not necessarily bring forth agreement or compliance.

5   Advising, recommending, providing answers or solutions: 'What you should do is ... Why don't you...? ... It would be best for you ... Let me suggest ...'

A depressed man doesn't usually want advice. Advice implies superiority and can make him feel inadequate and inferior.

6   Evaluating, judging, disapproving, blaming, criticizing: 'You are not thinking straight ... You are lazy, acting stupid ... Your clothes are horrible ...'

More than any other type of message, this makes a man feel inadequate, inferior, incompetent, bad or stupid. He is likely to become defensive, and communication will stop.

7   Praising, judging or evaluating positively, approving: 'You're a good man ... That's a really good thing to do ... I approve of ...'

Implies judgement, even though it is positive.

8   Supporting, reassuring, excusing, sympathizing: 'It's not so bad ... Don't worry ... You'll feel better ... '

To reassure a man may make him feel that you don't understand. Such messages convey that you don't accept unpleasant feelings and are uncomfortable with such feelings.

9   Diagnosing, psychoanalyzing, interpreting, offering insights: 'What you need is ... What's wrong with you is ... You're just trying to get attention ... You don't really mean that ... Your problem is ...'

To tell a man what he is really feeling, what his motives are, or why he feels as he does can be very threatening. If your analysis is wrong, he resists; if it is right, he can feel exposed, naked, trapped.

10   Questioning, probing, cross-examining, prying: 'Why...?, Who...?, What...?, Where...?, When...?, How...?'

This response can get a man talking and does have its place if used in moderation. Taken to the extreme, it can make him feel like he is on the witness stand. The best thing is to encourage him to talk spontaneously so that he says what he wants to say, and not what you want to hear.

11   Diverting, avoiding, by-passing, digressing, shifting: 'Let's not talk about that now ... Forget it ... That reminds me ...'

Such responses make a man feel you are not interested or that you don't want to understand. They communicate a lack of respect.

12 Kidding, teasing, making light of, joking, using sarcasm: 'Why don't you burn down the building? ... Got up on the wrong side of the bed?'

Such responses cut off communication and show a lack of respect. They often make a man angry or feel you don't understand how badly or seriously he feels about something.

EFFECTIVE ALTERNATIVES TO VERBAL ROADBLOCKS

1   Invite consideration: 'You have several options here ...'
2   Gentle caution: 'There are reasons to be cautious ...'
3   Consider responsibility: 'It sounds like you have many responsibilities ...'
4   Reflect value conflicts/choices: 'You need someone to talk to about your different choices ...'
5   Offer tentative suggestions: 'You could go in many different ways ...'
6   Assess behaviour: 'It takes courage to acknowledge problems ...'
7   Positive stroke from present position: 'I'd like to point out that you did a positive thing for yourself ...'
8   Validate feelings/hopeful directions: 'In your shoes it feels really hopeless right now ...'
9   Summarize issues: 'I sense that you want me to tell you what's wrong ...'
10 Lead to self-understanding: 'You are working to determine your feelings ...'
11 Acknowledge and face difficulty: 'It's a difficult subject for me to discuss, too ...'

Don't expect it to be easy to avoid verbal roadblocks. You won't be able to forget old habits and learn new ones overnight. Give yourself time. Remember that the first step is awareness. Start by recognizing when you make verbal roadblocks. Then gradually start to consider effective alternatives.

THE THINGS HE SAYS

It's often the case that when a man is depressed he'll repeat certain statements over and over again. It might be 'Why bother?' or 'I'm worthless,' or 'Who cares?' At times like these you are most likely to succumb to some of the verbal roadblocks mentioned above.

Consider what the man you care about says most often and, using the examples below, try to reframe your response so that it validates his emotional pain, reassures him, and keeps the lines of communication open between you.

If a man tells you he feels 'all alone':
Don't tell him he is not alone and lots of people including you care for him. Tell him, 'I know you feel alone now, but I'm glad to be with you. Is there anything I can do to help?'

If he says, 'Why bother? Life has no meaning anyway':
Don't remind him of all the things in his life he has to be grateful for. Tell him, 'I know you feel that life isn't worth living right now, but I want you to know that you matter to me. We'll work on this together.'

If he says, 'I'm a burden to you and everyone else':
Don't disagree. You could tell him that you know he feels like a burden and things aren't easy for both of you at the moment, but 'we'll get through this burdened feeling together.'

If he starts talking about ending his life:
Don't tell him he is crazy. Tell him how much you would miss him because he is important to you and you want him in your life for the long term.

If he tells you he feels expendable:
Don't tell him he is being stupid. Tell him you know he feels like that now, but you'll get through this empty feeling together.

When he tells you than nothing he does is ever any good and that he is a failure:

Don't disagree with him. Tell him that you know it is hard when things don't work out as planned, but you will get through the painful feelings of failure together.

When he tells you that he feels that he will never get better:
Don't tell him that nothing lasts for ever. Tell him you understand that it is frightening to be in such pain, but feelings come and go. 'We'll get through this together.'

6 Bringing Focus to the Dialogue

Using empathetic listening skills will encourage the man you care about to disclose the state of his feelings. But to avoid endless repetition and a feeling that you are not progressing, it's important to try and bring focus to your interactions. You can do this by helping him to identify the feelings, thoughts, options and alternatives that relate to the here and now.

It is crucial that you try to be specific and precise in your own statements and to seek clarification from him when he seems to use vague or ambiguous words. A man in crisis is overwhelmed, anxious and confused. He is coming from a point of feeling rather than thinking. Your role is to help him sort his feelings into manageable parts.

PINPOINT SPECIFIC FEELINGS

Help a man identify specific feelings and clarify what he feels. 'You seem upset' is a vague term that has many different meanings. 'You feel sad when this happens' helps him to identify the specific feeling of sadness. His anxiety levels should lessen if feelings are identified, explored and pinpointed, allowing him to address the crisis in a more positive manner.

See the feeling chart below for alternative words you can suggest.

Happy	Sad	Angry	Scared	Confused
Excited	Hopeless	Furious	Fearful	Bewildered
Elated	Sorrowful	Seething	Panicky	Trapped
Overjoyed	Depressed	Enraged	Afraid	Troubled
Delighted	Drained	Disgusted	Alarmed	Torn
Great	Lonely	Bitter	Petrified	Conflicted
Turned on	Miserable	Mad	Terrified	Pulled apart
Cheerful	Upset	Annoyed	Threatened	Disorganized
Up	Distressed	Frustrated	Insecure	Mixed up
Proud	Down	Agitated	Uneasy	Disturbed
Amused	Discouraged	Peeved	Worried	Blocked
Eager	Helpless	Resentful	Apprehensive	Frustrated
Glad	Sorry	Uptight	Timid	Bothered
Good	Lost	Dismayed	Unsure	Discomfort
Satisfied	Bad	Put out	Nervous	Undecided
Calm	Hurt	Disappointed	Tight	Uncertain
Content	Ashamed	Bugged	Tense	Puzzled

CHECK OUT ASSUMPTIONS

You may find that his own generalizations are reinforcing his sense of helplessness. A skill vital to focusing is the ability to be specific. For instance, if a man tells you, 'No one can help me,' it makes sense to ask what he means. Has he asked someone to help him? If so, who? Find out if he is making assumptions that there is no one to help.

ASK FOR CONCRETE EXAMPLES

If a man tells you he feels anxious about his job, it is appropriate to ask him what happened at work to lead him to feel this. Ask for examples that will either support his statements or clarify that he is making assumptions which can be explored.

RELATE TO THE HERE AND NOW

Often depressed men make global assumptions that may have been true in the past but are no longer true now. Always try and explore what is happening here and now, not what has happened in the past or is going to happen in the future.

USE BRIEF, ENCOURAGING RESPONSES

Brief, encouraging responses, rather than questions, can also help a depressed man elaborate, explain or take an in-depth look at his feelings and concerns. Examples include:

'Oh.' 'So.' 'And...' 'Um-hmm.'
The repetition of one or two key words he keeps using.
'Tell me more, give me an example.'
'Expand on that more. I don't quite get what you mean.'
'You feel ... because ...'
'This means a lot to you.'

Summarizing what is being said to you can also help a man to condense and crystallize what is going on in his head.

USE OPEN-ENDED QUESTIONS

Open-ended questions will also encourage him to explore his feelings. Open-ended questions are defined as questions that require more than a one-word answer. Queries that just require a 'Yes' or 'No' answer often serve as verbal roadblocks.

Open-ended questions often begin with *who, what, when* or *how*. It's best to avoid the why question 'Why did you do that?' because it is often met with resistance and defensiveness by the man.

Questions should encourage a man to express his feelings: 'How did you feel about this?' focuses on his concerns; 'What is concerning you right now?' explores what has been tried and projects new behaviour on what has been done before. Invite a man to tell more in his own way, and/or explore what might happen if a certain action were taken.

Remember, though, that balance is important. Too many questions can begin to seem like an interrogation. Try not to overuse open-ended questions.

Caring Confrontation

Confrontation aims to get at the real thoughts and feelings behind a man's depression. It may help him to attain better self-understanding or to move towards constructive behaviour. This is often best done by a qualified counsellor or therapist, but at certain times you might be able to use the approach. Certain responses invite caring confrontation when what you are hearing or seeing conflicts with what is being stated or revealed.

For instance:

When a man says he has no choices:
He needs to understand that there are always choices.
When a man feels helpless, or doesn't understand the difference between what he would like and what he needs to survive:
There are always options and these need to be explored.
When a man thinks others should anticipate his needs:
He needs to understand that he has to ask for what he wants and needs.
When a man thinks things should go his way all the time:
He needs to learn to negotiate what he wants.
When a man feels that negative emotions are bad:
He needs to appreciate that it is OK to feel bad.
When a man is making others feel guilty:
He needs to understand that no one changes unless they want to.

When a man feels he is responsible for the thoughts, actions and emotions of another:
He needs to understand that he can be concerned, but he is not responsible.
When he feels that because he loves, others should love him in return:
Others decide how they respond to his love.
If a man believes that relationships involve doing everything together:
He needs to learn that everyone has a need for independence and autonomy.
If a man believes he owns his partner or child:
He needs to understand that nobody owns anyone.
If a man says everything is fine and he clearly isn't:
He is in denial.
When a man believes that if someone loves him they won't be interested in anything else:
He needs to learn that love doesn't have to be all-consuming.
If a man thinks his opinion is fact:
He needs to understand that you can love someone and still disagree with them.
When a man believes the only option is to fight or be abusive to himself or others:
He needs to understand that war or violence is not the only way to state an opinion or resolve a situation.
When a man feels that he is a victim:
He has a distorted perception of his role.

The foundation for confrontation as an effective tool for helping is that helplessness is a learned state that can be unlearned. Thinking distortions make a man feel that he has no other options; your role is to make him aware of other alternatives and to pay attention to his thought processes.

In the words of Epictetus in the 1st century BC: 'Men are disturbed not by things, but by the view which they take of them.'

Or Aaron T Beck of this century: 'If we see things as negative, we are likely to feel negative and behave in a negative way.'

Once a man sees how negative he is being, he may be able to recognize that he is distorting reality and that there are positive alternatives, too. By supporting him, acknowledging his disappointment, reminding him that events in our lives are transitory and that there are always other options, you can help him reframe his perceptions.

The aim of caring confrontation is to encourage a man to see things differently. It's possible that the heart of his trouble is his viewpoint. If you can gently encourage him to explore other options, he may feel better and tackle the issue in a new way, which may achieve better results. For instance, if he tells you that he feels a failure because he didn't get the job he applied for, tell him:

You understand why he feels depressed: 'It must be hard when you don't get a job you want. No wonder you are upset.'
'You have had setbacks before and have always figured out creative solutions.'
'Not getting this job doesn't mean you won't ever get another job.'
'Not getting this job means you weren't right for that particular job; it doesn't mean you won't be right for another job.'

The best time to use caring confrontation is after a man feels accepted, valued and listened to. He will have begun to explore his feelings, and there will be an element of trust between you that makes him willing to hear your feedback.

When confronting and offering suggestions, you may find the following guidelines helpful:

- Listen actively, and confront him with his own feelings as you reflect them back.
- Give feedback. This is a specific, conscious description of his behaviour as you perceive it, and a statement of the effect it is having on you. Use 'I' messages: 'I hear you saying that.'

- State the facts without judgement: 'You say you regularly skip school ...'
- Get him to do the sorting out, to process the raw data, to think of what he can do.
- You may find that he uses indirect or manipulative communication to make you feel guilty or responsible for him, but always keep the issue on him, and don't take his pain upon yourself. His pain is not your pain. Focus on his concerns, not yours.
- Use tentative questioning: 'I'm wondering if ...?'
- You can help a man see things differently by raising possibilities and presenting options. You can give him a chance to see the positive side. Trying to be more optimistic is a technique that can be learned, and it is called cognitive therapy (see Chapter 10).

Remember, though, this kind of helping comes with a serious warning. You need to make sure you aren't manipulating the situation, telling him he is wrong or trying to cheer him up. And he won't even be ready to consider other options until you have made him feel accepted and valued. Also, remember that you can't learn skills from a book. If you want to practise them further, then you need to go on a counselling skills course.

Practical Help

Talking to a man who is depressed is not the only way you can help him. There are other ways you can give your support.

- Time is the greatest gift you can give anyone in this age of time-famine. Time makes a man feel that he is important. This time doesn't have always to be spent in activity or soul-searching. Simply watching TV together may help him.
- You could also occasionally offer to help him out with mundane tasks like washing up, tidying up, mowing the lawn, to encourage him to regain a sense of control over his life. If he asks for it, you

can support him by keeping him company if he is anxious about
going anywhere.

• Checking in with him on a regular basis may also be comforting.
It's particularly helpful when a man is depressed to speak with him
early in the morning and last thing at night when he feels most
vulnerable.

• You may want to help him out financially, but this tends to be
unwise. If you do want to help out, don't lend more than you are
happy to lose.

When a man you are helping wants you to help him practically,
you can support him, if that is what you want to do. Make
sure you are not moving towards action for its own sake and
that you are not pushing too hard or are unprepared. The
wrong kind of action right now could undermine everything
you have achieved so far. Take things slowly. Take the time
to discuss what he wants you to do to help him. Take the
time to think about how much you are prepared to help him,
and let him know what your limits are.

   Don't push him into action. Encourage him to act by offering
him support in what he wants to do, and don't take control of
what's happening. If problems occur, don't accuse him, but
gently investigate with him what went wrong. At all times,
remember that he needs to take control or he'll stay depressed.

Keeping the Lines of Communication Open

The following review tips and suggestions will help you keep
the lines of communication open.

1   Set aside regular time to talk. Limit interruptions and make sure
you are both comfortable and preferably and on equal footing. Try
not to discuss too many issues at once, and avoid confusing your
discussion with past history or other complaints. Make sure that
each of you gets time to talk.

2   Actively listen. This isn't always easy. Many of us have our own
     agendas and only hear what we want to hear. Don't interrupt until
     he has had his say. Make sure he knows that you accept what he
     says, and don't judge him in any way. Establishing eye contact
     helps remind him that he has your full attention and you are
     focused on what he is saying. If you tend to avert your eyes,
     remind yourself of the importance of eye contact. If he always
     looks down, don't force him to look up. Continue listening, and
     perhaps as you continue talking he will look up.
3   Open-ended questions open the way for discussion.
4   Mirroring and summarizing what he says communicates that you
     understand and respect him.
5   Separate who he is from what he does. If his behaviour has
     become unpredictable or his moods erratic, try to remind yourself
     of his character. Communicate to him that, even though he is
     depressed and you find this hard to deal with, you still value him.
     If he says or does anything to upset you, don't tell him he is being
     horrible, crazy or stupid. Tell him that when he says or does things
     like that you feel hurt, angry or anxious.
6   Observe not just what he says, but how he looks and moves and
     the tone of his voice. Watch for nonverbal clues, like slumped
     shoulders or hand-wringing, which tell you more about his
     emotional state than any words can. Under 10 per cent of our
     communication is based on words; around 90 per cent is based on
     nonverbal cues, like facial expression and body language. If you
     notice a sign that his emotions are near the surface – a heavy sigh
     or a shaky hand – signal to him that you accept that. Sit with him
     for as long as it takes; let him know it is fine to feel that way;
     don't tell him to put on a brave face; reach out and touch if you
     feel comfortable doing so; don't withdraw if he starts shouting. If
     you do all this he will realize that it isn't dangerous or unmanly to
     feel things. He will let his emotions out or, more typically, talk
     about how he feels. If you can help him understand that someone
     else understands what it is like to be him, he will experience
     feelings of self-worth and start to feel that perhaps he isn't so
     worthless or crazy after all.

7   Tell him that you care. Depending on the context of your relationship, tell him that you love and care for him. If it is appropriate, reach out and hold his hand, hug him, kiss him. He needs to know that you care about him. That he is still the same man he was before depression struck. Being more affectionate with him may help ease his anxiety. Studies show that touching, kissing and hugging have a healing power. Reaching out to hold his hand, cuddling or making love are all ways you can show him you care.

8   Use music. Remember that there are other ways to express your caring, apart from physical affection. Music can be a wonderful source of inspiration and healing, and is often used by therapists to aid recovery.

9   Random acts of kindness. Every now and then, write him a card, bring him some chocolates, take him for a meal. Random acts of kindness for no apparent reason may help pierce the gloom.

10   Reassure him of your permanence. He may not acknowledge it, but what a depressed man fears most of all is being abandoned by everyone, including you. Reassure him as often as you can that you know he feels bad right now, but the two of you will work through this together.

Sometimes you may be able to keep the lines of communication open and find ways to connect together. When intimate moments happen, cherish them. They will comfort both of you.

What to Do When He Rejects Your Help

What do you do if the man you care about rejects all your efforts, ignores them, or is hostile to you?

It's often the case that a severely depressed man will turn away offers of help and support. He may even become hostile towards you.

Research has shown that depressed men reject support more often than non-depressed men. A depressed man is likely to tell someone close to him that their advice won't help or that they do not understand what he is going through. There seems to be something inherent in depression that leads men to turn away help. The hopelessness and pessimism associated with depression often make seeking help seem futile. He is locked into thinking that nothing will help, so why bother. He may also reject help because he fears that accepting help from you will change the dynamic of your relationship, if he has always been the one in charge.

As discussed in Part 1, depressed men often ask for help in indirect ways, for instance, by displaying outbursts of temper, violence, overwork, alcohol and drug abuse. This indirect style of support-seeking makes it hard for you to know if he wants your help, and how best to help. If he rejects your help, this makes you defensive. If you withdraw from him, he feels more alone. How do you know when to support him and when to back off?

Finding a way to help him is difficult, but there are things you can do:

- Accept that he doesn't want your help. Don't take it personally. His rejection is not of you; rather, it reflects that he is depressed and has problems receiving and asking for help.
- Think about how you feel. Are you sad, frustrated, angry or feeling helpless? Work on coping with these feelings first. Once you have identified how you feel, be optimistic about making changes. You may decide that the atmosphere is too charged and it would benefit all concerned if you left the helping to someone else. Or you may want to consider ways to improve how you offer support. Most of these ways will have been mentioned in this chapter already, but there are certain things that need to be re-emphasized when help is constantly rejected.

- Perhaps there are other ways for him to acknowledge his feelings, if talking doesn't work. You might encourage him to write down, paint or draw how he feels. A mood diary or a daily record of his feelings, for instance, can help someone who is depressed. The internet has much appeal for men suffering from depression and anxiety. There are now thousands of websites specifically about suicide, and many more about depression. The anonymity of the internet appeals to many men, and it can be a source of comfort and relief; the danger is that it can isolate them from real relationships further. Do be aware that without any policing some of the material a man comes into contact with on the internet may make him feel worse, not better.

- Reassure him of your permanence. Continuing to offer unqualified support if he needs it will be very hard when your help is constantly turned away. It's easy to feel like giving up. But remind yourself of how beneficial social support is when a man gets depressed.

- Be realistic. You can't lift his depression from him. No one can do that. You do not have to have an answer for every difficulty he has.

- Keep a routine going. Try to keep your life as regular as possible. Don't drop out of your usual activities or isolate yourself from other people. His turning down your help may make you feel resentful, frustrated or angry if you are not doing something else with your life.

- Tell him how you feel when he rejects your support. Without accusing him or blaming him, share your feelings with him. He may be unaware that he is excluding your help. Ask him if there is a specific way you can be of help to him.

- Work as a team. This is never more important than when you are trying to improve the communication process. You must work together in providing support for each other. It wouldn't hurt to ask him occasionally for his support and advice. You may be surprised to see that he can help even when he is depressed, and that being useful makes him feel better.

- Ask others for help. Caring for a depressed man is an unsettling task. It can be even more unnerving when your help is rejected. Take care of yourself, and let other people help you. Don't make the mistake of thinking you can do it all by yourself. You can't.

A lot of information has been given in this chapter, and it may take you a while to absorb it. You may want to re-read this chapter at some point.

Remind yourself that, in certain cases, help from a doctor, counsellor, therapist, psychologist, psychiatrist or mental health expert may be required. Chapters 8 and 10 will discuss the various treatment options available and how to encourage a man to seek these treatments. If, however, the man you care about has the blues or mild depression, he may not need treatment at all. As discussed, the blues differ from depression because a man is still able to consider your suggestions and take actions that will make him feel better. There are ways he can help himself feel better and that you can encourage him to feel better, and we'll explore these next.

7

Helping Him When He's Feeling Blue

How to gain, how to keep and how to recover happiness is in fact for most men at all times the secret motive for all they do and of all they are willing to endure.

William James

If the man you care about is feeling blue, there are ways to prevent a downward spiral into depression.

Of course, urging him to cheer up or pull himself together is not a good idea. If he isn't ready to do that, he will feel unaccepted and pressured. He'll also suppress his emotions, and his problems may never get solved. But what if he has acknowledged his feelings and thought through the issues and wants to feel more positive? How can you help?

You might try the following suggestions. The ideas apply to both the blues and depression, but bear in mind that when a man is feeling blue, he is more amenable to distractions and suggestions to make him feel better.

Have More Fun

It may sound obvious, but happiness requires action. Find out what he enjoys, and suggest he try to do at least one enjoyable thing a day, such as visiting friends, listening to a CD, taking a brisk walk, spending an hour watching the sky, reading a good book, watching a video, spending time with the children, spending time with you, feeding the birds or squirrels, having a hot bath, ringing up a friend, doing a jigsaw, buying a small treat, helping someone else and so on.

Research has shown that laughter can actually ease stress and anxiety. The positive emotions associated with laughter decrease stress hormones and increase the number of certain immune cells. If you can encourage him to see the lighter side of things, he may just find that laughter really can work wonders.

Diversions

Entertainment that can divert him may have its place. You might like to take him to the cinema or the theatre. Comedies, musicals or action adventures are often best. Listening to music, singing songs or going to concerts can have a healing quality. You could go to a sporting event together. You could buy him a really great book to read. You could watch an entertaining video together.

You might to want to take him out for a meal, or cook his favourite meal as a surprise. Shopping trips can also help eradicate the blues. Food and 'retail therapy' can be excellent distractions as long as they are not taken to the extreme. Playing favourite card games or board games together may also be diverting.

Encouraging him to do small chores that can take his mind off his worries may also eradicate the blues. Washing his car, gardening, painting, odd jobs around the house or baking can all provide him with a sense of completion and control.

Volunteering to help others can remind him that there are others in need, too, and divert him from his own concerns. If he is up to it, social gatherings or simply getting together with friends and family to hear their news can be a good distraction.

As long as diversion doesn't become avoidance, an element of escapism can help.

Social Network

A man's life finds meaning not only through how he feels about himself but in his relationships with others. All human beings need relationships with others to feel contented. No man is an island. He needs others to be happy, and he needs many kinds of relationships to feel fulfilled.

Research proves that social ties may help men cope better with stress. Men who are happy in their relationships with others tend to be less anxious and stressed. He may be the kind of man who prefers his own company, and if this is the case don't force him. He needs to find what makes him feel good, but, however much of a loner he is, gently remind him that he develops as a man through his emotional connection with others and that, throughout his life, relationships will be very important.

Encourage Him to Be More Interested in His Health

Fear and ignorance lead most men to suffer in silence when their health is poor. Fear and ignorance also lead most men to suffer in silence when they feel depressed.

Encouraging the man you care about to take a more active interest in his health and well-being will help. If he won't talk about it, try leaving books and leaflets around, or the numbers for medical helplines. Make them available without badgering him.

In the meantime, it wouldn't hurt for you to be better informed should there be a problem with his health that causes him anxiety. Here are the most common questions men would ask their doctor, if only they were brave enough to go, and which tend to cause them the greatest anxiety:

I'm terrified of getting testicular cancer. How can I prevent it?
Testicular cancer is the most common cancer in men aged 20 to 35. Cases have doubled in the last two years, and no one knows why. If caught early, 96 per cent of cases can be treated successfully. Self-examination is the best defence. Tell him to check his testicles for lumps, enlargements, heaviness in the scrotum or a sudden collection of fluid in it, or a dull ache in the abdomen or groin. If he is concerned, suggest you visit his doctor together. Treatment involves surgery and, if the cancer spreads, chemotherapy. In most cases, sex life and fertility are not affected.

Who's at risk of prostate cancer, and how do I know if I have it?
Around 95 per cent of sufferers are 45 and older, and in the next 20 years prostate cancer is set to become more common than lung cancer in the UK. Prostate cancer often develops silently, but he should be vigilant for problems such as difficulty or delays in urinating, having to use the restroom frequently, blood in the urine and pain and stiffness in the lower back and hips. Rectal examination, ultrasound and blood tests can diagnose prostate cancer. Treatment includes surgery, radiotherapy and hormone treatment. There is a risk of long-term impotence. For more information on male cancers, contact Everyman (see Resources chapter).

What can I do about my embarrassing smelly feet?
He should get rid of smelly trainers and wear cotton or wool socks and leather shoes – natural fibres will let his feet breathe and the sweat evaporate. Man-made fabrics like nylon and fake leather don't let your feet breathe. Trainers can be the worst culprits, because they are synthetic and full of insulation. He should ensure that he buys new ones frequently and doesn't leave them on for

long periods of time. You might want to suggest that he bathes his feet in warm water with tea tree oil, which has anti-bacterial properties – the smell is actually caused by bacteria which thrives on sweat – and use a pumice stone to remove dead skin, which makes the problem worse. He should also check between his toes for fungal infections and, if necessary, visit his pharmacist for deodorant spray or powder and anti-fungal medicines.

Will I get a heart attack if I keep losing my temper?

Yes, he is more likely to get a heart attack if he doesn't learn to calm down. Men with a short fuse are three times more likely to have a heart attack than the calmer members of the population, as are drinkers and smokers. Research suggests that the hormones released into your blood when you are angry could cause blood clots which block the heart. So, along with eating a low-fat diet rich in fruit and vegetables, regular exercise and avoiding smoking and drinking, men should try to avoid stress and anger by learning to relax more and being less competitive.

What can I do when I start losing my hair?

Hair loss in men, especially over the age of 30, is very common. Ageing and male hormones are to blame. There is no way to prevent baldness, but simple measures like gently massaging the scalp to increase blood flow to the hair follicles, washing the hair with a mild shampoo and towelling it dry may help. Hair dryers, vigorous rubbing and tugging at tangles should be avoided. Gentleness is the key. Over-the-counter remedies which stimulate hair re-growth in men can have serious side-effects and should only be taken under medical supervision.

Is my beer gut bad for my health?

Without a doubt, beer bellies are bad for men. Men tend to put on weight around their abdomen and, according to experts, apple-shaped men are more at risk of heart disease and heart attacks than those who are more pear-shaped, because the fat is closer to their vital organs. He should cut down on alcohol – it will give him a beer gut. He should also eat more fruits and vegetables, as well as carbohydrates such as pasta and rice, and take regular exercise.

For more information, contact the British Heart Foundation (see Resources chapter).

How can I stop excessive sweating?

Daily washing, shaving under his armpits – the hair under the armpits acts as a breeding ground for the bacteria that make sweat smelly – and asking his pharmacist for an antibacterial lotion may help.

Why do I sometimes feel like life isn't worth living?

Assure him that he is not alone. Depression is commonplace among men. If he can't pull through his negative mood, encourage him to see his doctor, who may refer him to a counsellor.

What should I do if I get a sexually-transmitted disease?

Sexually-transmitted diseases (STDs) are increasing in men, and there is a lot of ignorance about them. Genital herpes and chlamydia cases are rising dramatically. To prevent the spread of STDs, he should always use a condom. If he notices any of the following symptoms – a yellow discharge from his penis, inflammation of the testicles, irritation of his penis, pain when urinating – he should seek help from his doctor or the nearest genito-urinary clinic, which will be listed in the phone book.

I can't get an erection anymore – will my sex drive return?

A man needs to understand that he can love someone and still lose his libido. If you are his partner, you need to understand that he can still love you but be unable to have an erection. It's difficult, but try not take his loss of libido personally – that will just make him feel worse. Reassure him of your affection and find other ways to be intimate without intercourse. Every man's interest in sex goes through highs and lows in his life. In most cases it's temporary, but there could be an underlying problem, such as depression. Medications such as antidepressants, tranquilizers and heart drugs can flatten sex drive, as can stress, poor health and the arrival of a new baby. Drinking can cause a loss of libido, or even impotence. If a man is really concerned, suggest he visit his doctor for any medications or treatments that might help. Relate (National Marriage Guidance Council) offers counselling for couples, while the Impotence Association runs a helpline and website (see Resources chapter).

Tests a Man Should Consider

IN HIS TWENTIES

- He should check his weight every few months, and seek advice if it significantly rises or falls.
- He should check his testicles regularly for lumps. This is the age for testicular cancer which is curable if caught early.
- He should have his blood pressure checked a few times.
- He should have a urine test for protein at least once, as protein in the urine can signal kidney problems.

IN HIS THIRTIES AND FORTIES

- He should check his weight as in his twenties.
- Every three to five years he should have checks on blood pressure, cholesterol, and urine for protein and sugar (for kidney problems and diabetes).

IN HIS FIFTIES AND OVER

- He should check his weight as in his twenties.
- He should have an eye test for glaucoma.
- Every three years he should have his blood pressure, cholesterol and urine checked.
- Some experts think he should have a prostate test for prostate cancer, his faeces checked for bowel cancer, and have a heart recording while exercising as an early indicator of heart disease.

Depending on any symptoms he may have, a doctor may advise chest X-rays, tests for anaemia, kidney or liver function, tests of breathing efficiency, testosterone and bone density. If his parents or siblings had heart trouble, his cholesterol levels may be tested. The same goes for glaucoma and bowel cancer.

Exercise

Exercise has many health benefits, not least of which is helping to lift and prevent depression. Exercise is also something you and the man you care about can do together.

Regular exercise may be more effective at beating the blues than medication, according to new research. Recent studies show that aerobic exercise such as running, walking, dancing, biking, swimming, hiking and so on, and non-aerobic exercise such as weight-training and sprinting, can alleviate the symptoms of mild to moderate depression. Even low-intensity exercise such as walking can help.

Simply engaging in regular exercise may be all that a man who is feeling blue needs. And exercise can be so effective at lifting the symptoms of depression that it is often recommended alongside counselling or medical treatments. Just half an hour of brisk activity three times a week may be enough to keep symptoms at bay, and the more exercise a man does, the more he reduces the chances of depression returning.

Why is exercise such a powerful weapon in the fight against depression? There are several explanations. On a psychological level it can distract a man from painful feelings and give him a feeling of mastery and control, to help him combat feelings of hopelessness. If the exercise involves teamwork, it can make a man feel less isolated. Exercise that takes place outdoors, like walking in the woods, hiking or rowing, can be beneficial on a spiritual as well as emotional level, bringing a sense of oneness with nature.

Biological sources could also explain the positive benefits of exercise. Physical activity promotes the release of chemicals in the brain called endorphins, which reduce the experience of pain and create feelings of elation. Activity also improves the action of neurotransmitters such as serotonin, which are essential for mood regulation.

The man in your life may have some misconceptions about exercise. Exercise is not dangerous if you do it safely and regularly. It is not just for young men; it can benefit any man, whatever his age, as long as the exercise is tailored to his age. Nor does he need to invest in designer equipment. A brisk walk in the park costs nothing.

If you can encourage the man you care about to take more exercise, it could make all the difference. You may find that he has a hard time getting active, so focus on small steps first. A short walk, taking the stairs instead of the lift – anything is better than nothing. Don't try to force him to move, though. Exercise can only help him if he is willing to participate in it. You might suggest forms of exercise that seem more like fun if he is reluctant to commit to a regular routine – the odd game of tennis, or a swim, or a game of football, for instance. If he has never exercised before, make sure that he engages in friendly, non-competitive activities at first. Feeling unfit or inadequate at sport can trigger bouts of low self-esteem.

If he wants to get going, how much exercise is enough? Most fitness and health experts recommend a programme of aerobic exercise three to five times a week for 30 to 60 minutes, with 5 to 10 minutes before and after to warm up and cool down. Strength-training to tone the muscles and firm the body should take place three to four times a week, with rest days in between. The activity should be challenging but not so difficult as to make him feel a sense of failure or inferiority. It should also be varied and fun.

Improved muscle tone can also lead to improved posture. When a man is feeling down he often tends to stoop, with his head down and shoulders rounded, as if he is carrying the weight of the world on his shoulders. He may feel better if he breathes deeply, carries his head high and stands tall.

When using exercise to alleviate symptoms of depression, avoid overtraining. A man may become addicted to the elevated mood state that exercise produces, but exercising too much weakens, not strengthens, the body. Signs for you to be alert to are anxiety about missing workouts, increased rigidity about workout times, relegating work, family and friends to secondary status for the sake of a workout, and recurrent injuries and fatigue.

Exercise can combat depression. Exercise is a good thing. But you can have too much of a good thing. Moderation is key.

Food and Mood

A good diet is one in which the food a man eats contains the nutrients he needs to promote physical, mental and emotional health. A bad diet can contribute to problems such as obesity, heart disease, cancer, digestive disorders, mood swings, irritability and insomnia – to name but a few.

Just when a balanced, wholesome diet is needed most, men who are suffering from depression often neglect their body's needs. He may have no appetite at all, or he may crave unhealthy and fattening foods. As a result, nutritional deficiencies or imbalances are likely, particularly a lack of B vitamins, folic acid, vitamin C and the minerals calcium, copper, iron, magnesium and potassium. Malnourishment or weight problems clearly contribute to moods spiralling downwards.

More and more research is linking what we eat to how we feel. In her book *Food and Mood*, dietician Elizabeth Somer explores how the foods we eat can heighten depression. She believes that certain eating habits, like skipping meals or having erratic eating habits, aggravate negative moods. Somer advises five to six small meals and snacks spread throughout the day.

Dr Judith Wurtman, a researcher at the Massachusetts Institute of Technology, believes that carbohydrates alter mood because they release insulin, which encourages the production of serotonin. Higher serotonin levels are thought to be linked with improved mood. Carbohydrate-rich foods have an effect similar to that of some antidepressant medication.

Don't be surprised if the man you care about suddenly starts eating large amounts of high-sugar foods. He may be using these foods as a form of self-medication. The problem with this is that the effects tend to be short term, and if he eats too much of the wrong kind of carbohydrate he will gain weight and put his health at risk.

Somer advises that a carbohydrate-rich snack such as whole-grain breads and cereals or starchy vegetables such as a potato or a sweet potato should be planned for that time of the day when a man feels most vulnerable. She suggests that cravings not be avoided, but responded to in moderation and with planned, nutritious foods.

The relationship between the brain's chemistry and different nutrients is unclear, but nutritional guidelines from the Department of Health offer pointers on nutrition for sufferers of depression. Plenty of whole grains, peas and lentils and other pulses, and regular amounts of lean meat, oily fish, shellfish and eggs will supply B vitamins, iron, potassium, magnesium, copper and zinc. A high intake of fresh fruit and vegetables (such as asparagus, broccoli, cabbage, melon, oranges and berries) will supply ample vitamin C. Dark green leafy vegetables will improve levels of calcium, magnesium and iron. Dried fruits will provide potassium and iron, while dairy produce (preferably low-fat) will boost levels of calcium. These recommendations can be kept in mind when considering the general guidelines for good diet.

What Is a Good Diet for a Man?

In general, a man's diet should contain a balanced mix of carbohydrates, proteins and fats. He should also be eating enough fibre, ensuring that he gets an adequate intake of essential vitamins and minerals, and drinking lots of water.

CARBOHYDRATE

The World Health Organization (WHO) recommends that between 50 and 70 per cent of a person's diet should be carbohydrate. Carbohydrate is found in bread, pasta, rice, potatoes, pulses, nuts and seeds, fruits, vegetables and salads. He should have five servings of fruit, vegetables or salad a day, and four servings of carbohydrates from other sources. (A serving is one piece of fruit, one slice of bread, one medium jacket potato, etc.)

PROTEIN

Protein should make up around 15 per cent of his diet. Protein is found in meats, dairy produce, eggs, fish, poultry, pulses, nuts and seeds. He should try to have two servings a day of non-dairy proteins, and one serving a day of a dairy product.

FAT

Fats should make up between 25 and 30 per cent of his diet. Fats are found in most foods. Too much of the wrong sort of fat is bad for him. Avoid saturated fats from animal produce, and fats that are solid at room temperature, like lard and butter. Fats that are liquid at room temperature, i.e. vegetable oils, are far preferable since they don't contain the chemicals that can clog arteries.

FIBRE

An adequate intake of dietary fibre is also important. WHO recommends around 30 g of fibre a day. Foods high in fibre include fruits and vegetables, brown bread, rice and pasta, high-fibre cereals, potatoes and baked beans. A jacket potato contains around 5 to 8 grams of fibre.

Fibre swells the bulk of the food residue in the intestine and helps to soften it by increasing the amount of water retained. It is vital to the health of the digestive system; ailments such as irritable bowel, constipation and piles result if a man doesn't get enough fibre. Western diets are often low in fibre, and men who eat a lot of processed and refined foods are vulnerable. But there are easy ways to boost fibre:

- Have a bowl of high-fibre cereal for breakfast.
- Eat brown bread, pasta and rice.
- Snack on fruits and nuts rather than crisps and chocolate.

High-fibre foods are nutritious and can satisfy without being fattening. Some types of fibre – those found in vegetables and fruits and oats – can reduce blood cholesterol. Cholesterol is a variety of fat that has some health benefits, so it shouldn't be excluded from a diet, but too much cholesterol is linked to clogging of the arteries – especially those around the heart.

VITAMINS AND MINERALS

Vitamins and minerals are also vital for a man's health. When there is a deficiency, he may suffer from a range of health problems which undermine his well-being but are not normally treated by doctors. If he eats a wide variety of foods he should get all the nutrients he needs. However, even fresh whole foods can be less nutritious than you think. Nutrients can be leaked from our food in a variety of hidden ways, and chemicals are often added.

Foods most at risk of nutrient deficiency are pre-prepared or processed foods, and foods that have been frozen and canned. In addition, alcohol, drugs, tobacco, stress and environmental pollution can deplete the body of essential nutrients. For all these reasons you might what to suggest to him that he tries to buy organic, eats as much fresh whole food as he can, and supplements his diet with extra vitamins and minerals.

Common Vitamins	Good for	Found in
Vitamin A	Skin and eyes	Liver, carrots, green vegetables
Vitamin B	Nervous system and circulation	Marmite, bread, breakfast cereals, dairy products, vegetables
Vitamin C	Immune system and iron absorption	Citrus fruits, vegetables, potatoes, green vegetables
Vitamin D	Bones and teeth	Oily fish, salmon, dairy produce
Vitamin E	Fat metabolism and nervous system	Nuts, seeds, vegetable oils

Common Minerals	Good for	Found in
Calcium	Bones, teeth and blood clotting	Milk, cheese, broccoli
Chromium	Sugar metabolism and blood pressure regulation	Egg yolk, wheatgerm, chicken
Copper	Healthy connective tissues	Most foods
Iron	Blood, circulatory and immune systems	Liver, dried fruit, meat, green vegetables
Magnesium	Muscles and nervous system	Nuts, chicken, cheese

Potassium	Nerve transmission and acid/alkaline balance in the body	Raisins, potatoes, fruit, vegetables
Selenium	Heart and liver	Kidney, liver, red meat
Zinc	Reproductive system, hair and nails	Cheese, wholemeal bread, eggs

Vitamins A, C and E and the mineral selenium are also anti-oxidants, which means they can help the body remove harmful toxins.

Warning: Always consult a doctor or pharmacist if vitamin or mineral supplements are taken. Some – vitamin A, for instance – can be harmful if taken in large amounts.

Dietary Supplements	Good for
Evening primrose oil	Skin and regulating cholesterol and blood pressure levels
Fish oils	Heart and promoting mental agility
Garlic	Lungs and immune system
Ginseng	Mental health and stamina
Lecithin	Heart and circulatory system
Royal Jelly	Stamina and energy levels

WATER

The chances are he is not drinking enough water, an important part of a man's diet – it keeps him hydrated and helps flush toxins out of the body. Ideally he should be drinking at least six to eight glasses of water a day to maintain health.

What to Avoid

ALCOHOL

Gently encourage him to cut down on alcohol. Alcohol is high in calories and depletes the body of essential nutrients. Also, when a man is feeling blue he may be more vulnerable to alcohol addiction. Alcohol is not inherently harmful, if limited to 2–3 units a day, but it can get out of hand for one in twenty men. If this is the case, he should aim for sensible drinking and set a limit to the amount he drinks. The British Medical Association recommends a limit of 21 units for men a week. A unit of alcohol is the equivalent of a small glass of wine, half a pint of beer or a single whisky or gin. Encourage him to think about how drink can affect his health, his sex life and his self-esteem. He shouldn't worry about the occasional binge as long as he returns to modest consumption afterwards. If he needs more serious help with alcohol or if he is addicted to drugs or other dangerous substances, see Chapter 10.

SALT

Moderation in salt is also advised. Excessive intakes of salt can promote fluid retention and cause a rise in blood pressure, and an increased risk of stroke, heart disease and kidney failure. Much processed food contains salt. Crisps are high in salt, and lots of men sprinkle salt on their vegetables, which isn't necessary.

SUGAR

Refined white sugar is also bad for his health. It rots his teeth, sends his blood-sugar levels up, affects his mood and makes him gain weight. Most men aren't as passionate about chocolate as women are, but if he has a sweet tooth, suggest that he eat fruit rather than sweets, biscuits and cakes.

CAFFEINE

Too much caffeine (more than four cups of coffee or six cups of tea a day) may also not be a good idea. It can give the man you care about a quick apparent burst of energy, but can also lead to fatigue and low moods. If he is a coffee addict, suggest that he cut back slowly until he has no more than two cups a day. He should be aware that headaches and lethargy, which are symptoms of caffeine withdrawal, can last one to three days before real improvements are felt.

If He Can't Cook

Even if a man can't cook or won't cook, there are simple ways he can improve his diet.

He can think about the choices he makes. If he understands that chips are going to make him get a beer gut, he may decide to have a jacket potato instead. His typical food intake may look like this:

Breakfast	Danish pastry and cappuccino, or bacon, eggs and sausage
Lunch	McDonalds and fries with a chocolate bar, or meat pie and chips
Dinner	Curry, rice, poppadoms and pickles, or a take-away deep-crust pepperoni pizza, washed down with beer

Suggest to him that he might feel considerably healthier if he tried these alternatives:

Breakfast	Bowl of high-fibre cereal with orange juice, or scrambled eggs on toast
Lunch	Chicken salad sandwiches, without mayonnaise, and fruit
Dinner	Pasta with simple vegetable sauce

Try to encourage him to increase his percentage of complex carbo-hydrates, fibre, vitamins and mineral by eating more vegetables, fruits and grains. Depression has been linked to vitamin B_6 deficiency, so perhaps he could think about eating food rich in vitamin B_6 such as bananas, skinless chicken, dark leafy greens, oatmeal and potatoes.

Is he drinking enough? He may be feeling low because he is dehydrated. Suggest he drinks six 8-oz/225-ml glasses of water a day to correct this.

If he understands how fat can go straight to his belly, he might start getting more interested in the fat content of foods by reading food labels or choosing dishes that are low-fat, and boiled or grilled rather than fried. He should try to make sure his diet is no more than 30 per cent fat.

If he lives off toast, he could make sure he chooses wholemeal bread. Beans on toast is an excellent nutritious meal. Having oily fish such as pilchards on toast is, too. Oily fish contain many of the oils that can pre-vent heart disease.

If he likes his takeaway pizza, he might order a thin and crusty one rather than deep crust, and choose a vegetable topping rather than pep-peroni. If he likes an Indian, suggest that he stick to dry cooked meats and vegetables, and go slow with the poppadoms and pickles. If he likes Chinese, suggest he try vegetable dishes and choose rice in preference to noodles.

Try to encourage him to eat a big breakfast, a moderate lunch and a light supper with a few snacks in between. Explain to him that eating large meals at night, when the body needs to rest, doesn't make sense. You don't fill up a car with petrol and then park it in the garage.

Explain to him how important breakfast is. Breakfast gives him energy to start the day, helps stabilize blood sugars, lifts his mood and helps him think more clearly. He should try to make sure his breakfast includes one serving each of grains, fruit and low-fat dairy products. This boosts energy and improves mood.

Remind him how sleepy he feels after a heavy lunch, and suggest that he eats moderately at midday.

If he has lost his appetite because he is anxious and unhappy, gently urge him to consider a well-balanced vitamin and mineral supplement.

You can't force a man to eat right, unless you are completely in charge of his diet. All you can do is give him the information he needs to decide for himself. Try not to lecture him, just gently confront him with the logic: he is what he eats. Help him recognize that the food he eats affects his mood and health as well as his waistline. Tell him you are concerned about his health. More often than not, you will see him make changes to his diet.

If he wants to explore the matter further, you might want to suggest that he visit a nutritional therapist. Nutritional therapists use diet, vitamin and mineral supplementation to balance the body and mind and prevent illness.

Finally, depending on whether or not you are living together, you might want to consider making these lifestyle changes too. You can be his partner in positive change.

The Spare Tyre

If the man you care about is overweight or has a spare tyre, losing weight will improve his self-esteem and mood, but he may be at such a low point that he can't be bothered or can't get motivated. Once again, presenting him with the facts may give him the motivation he needs.

Heart disease is one of the two major causes of death. Men are most affected by heart trouble. Many experts believe that diet is the major explanation.

Western men are eating too much of the wrong kinds of food. There is an epidemic of obesity. Obesity increases the risk, not just of heart disease, but also of high blood pressure, diabetes, fatigue, skin rashes, tooth decay and arthritis. Men's diets are too high in fat, sugar and salt, and too low in fibre (which also predisposes men to bowel cancer), and too low in vitamin E, an antioxidant that removes free radicals from the body – free radicals are by-products of metabolism and appear to be linked with heart disease.

When men eat more than they need, extra weight tends go around the waist – as opposed to the hips, which is where most women gain fat. Fat gained round the waist corresponds to fat accumulated within the abdominal cavity. This centrally-held fat appears most important in generating health problems. It is more unhealthy to be apple-shaped than pear-shaped. High alcohol intake also tends to produce fat around the abdomen, rather than the backside, for reasons experts aren't really sure of. This is what brings about the familiar 'beer belly'.

Bear in mind that a man may be big or weigh a lot on the scales, but not be overweight. Weight alone is not a reliable indicator of physical condition, it's the amount of fat a man is carrying that is important. His weight may be mainly muscle. You can probably tell if he is carrying too much fat, but if you are not sure you might want to try to work out his Body Mass Index (BMI), which relates height to weight. The formula is this: weight in kilograms divided by his height in metres squared. If the index is above 30, he is overweight and his health is at risk.

Hopefully, once a man understands the serious risk to his health that excess fat presents, he may be willing to adjust his diet and lifestyle to lose weight. The first thing he needs to do is determine if he is overweight. The table below will help you. He should also consult with his doctor.

Height	Acceptable Range	Obese
1.6m/5'3"	52–65kg/8st3–10st3	78kg/12st5
1.62m/5'4"	53–66kg/8st5–10st5	79kg/12st6
1.66m/5'5"	55–69kg/8st11–10st12	83kg/13st
1.7m/5'7"	58–73kg/9st2–11st7	88kg/13st12
1.76m/5'9"	62–77kg/9st10–12st2	92kg/14st7
1.8m/5'10¹/₂"	65–80kg/10st3–12st8	96kg/15st2
1.84m/6'	67–84kg/10st8–13st3	101kg/16st
1.9m/6'2"	73–90kg/11st7–14st2	108kg/17st
1.92m/6'4"	75–93kg/11st11–14st10	112kg/17¹/₂st

Helping Him Lose Weight

To lose weight, the formula is simple: reduce food intake and increase activity.

As a guide, men aged between 19 and 60 who are moderately active need around 2,550 calories a day – but do remember that each man is different, with different energy requirements. Rather than focusing on calories, it is far better to encourage him to focus on making nutritious food choices like those mentioned in the previous section. This will ensure steady and gradual weight loss. In fact, don't even mention the word *diet* – this will conjure up images of low-fat yogurt and broccoli. He simply needs to cut down his portion sizes and ensure that he gets all his nutrients from the four main food groups:

1   Meat, fish, eggs and pulses
2   Milk, cheese and calcium-rich foods
3   Fruit and vegetables
4   Cereals – including bread, pasta and rice.

If a man is eating to lose weight, his diet should have increased amounts of carbohydrates like pasta, rice, potatoes and wholegrain bread. He should eat plenty of fresh fruit and vegetables – at least five servings a day. Fibre intake should come from vegetable products, high-fibre breads and fruits. He should have 30 g of fibre a day. His fat intake should be no more than 25 per cent. He should choose fat sources containing low cholesterol that are high in polyunsaturated fats, as in fish, nuts and vegetable oils such as sunflower or olive oil. He should try to avoid animal fats, dripping, bacon, sausages, hard margarines, pastries and cakes, and select reduced-fat milk and dairy products.

The World Health Organization recommends moderation in salt intake. Salt is found in crisps, snacks and processed foods. He should not automatically pour salt over his food, and should try to choose foods low in sugar. He should ensure he drinks enough water and gets all the essentials vitamins and minerals, preferably from the foods he eats. Nutrients are better absorbed from foods than from a pill.

He may be impatient to see results, but crash diets or fad diets only result in fluid loss. If he wants to lose weight and keep it off, he should aim for no more than one or two pounds a week. If that sounds too wimpish, remind him that over three months he will lose a stone. It took a while for him to get a pot belly; it will take a while to lose it.

Here are some tips that might help him stay on track. And always suggest that he sees a doctor or seeks professional advice before embarking on a new diet and exercise routine.

- Perhaps you or a friend with weight to lose could diet with him and help him persevere.
- Prepare him for the fact that he may teased if he starts being careful about his food intake, especially by other men. Dieting is considered to be a woman's thing. Remind him that he will be the one visiting his mates when they have their heart attack.
- Help him understand that what he puts into his mouth affects his weight, health and his mood. He is what he eats.
- Suggest that he supplement his new eating habits with regular exercise – three 30-minute walks a week is a good place to start.
- Work out a target weight, and aim for a steady weight loss of $1/2$–1 pound a week.
- Suggest that he write down his food intake so that he can see how nutritious his diet is.
- Suggest he eat a balanced diet with lots of variety.
- Suggest he eat little and often.
- Suggest that he eat well at breakfast and lunch, but lightly in the evening. If possible he should stop eating altogether after 8 p.m.
- Suggest that he use smaller plates, eat more slowly, and avoid eating in front of the TV or doing anything else which can take his mind off what he is eating.

- Think of a reward for his efforts – though your approval and the approval of others may be enough.

Quitting Smoking

If the man you care about smokes, here are some facts you might like to discuss with him:

- 40 per cent of smokers die from smoking-related diseases such as lung cancer, heart disease and cancer of the bladder, stomach, mouth and throat.
- Non-smokers live longer than smokers.
- The skin of smokers ages faster.
- The children of smokers get more respiratory infections.
- Other people can get lung cancer from passive smoking.
- Smokers get indigestion and ulcers.
- Smoking robs his body of essential nutrients.
- Smoking makes him feel tired and moody.

If he is feeling blue, he may become even more dependent on smoking to lift his mood and now might not be the time to give up, but if he can make the effort he will be taking the biggest single step possible towards his future health. He may try and fail, like the majority of smokers. Remind him that tomorrow is another day.

If he needs help with quitting there are lots of books, leaflets, support groups and videos that can help him. Giving up smoking should be planned in several stages. He should prepare to give up and set the day. He should smoke his last cigarette and get rid of ashtrays, lighters, matches and unused cigarettes. A supply of low-sugar chewing gum or sweets will help him when cravings start. He should avoid smoke-filled environments and keep as occupied as he can. Nicotine patches, gums or inhalers may help. When the going gets tough, remind him that the urge to smoke will pass.

Light Therapy

If the man you care about is one of the millions who suffer from seasonal affective disorder (SAD), scientists now believe his condition is related to how much light hits the retina of the eye. The less light, the more melatonin (a sleep hormone) circulates in the body. Melatonin affects serotonin levels in the body, and lowered serotonin levels are thought to be linked to depression.

Getting as much light as possible during the spring and summer months will slow the production of melatonin. Bigger windows and a south- or east-facing house, cutting back trees to admit more light, painting walls white, having light-coloured floors, and adding more intense lighting such as halogen lamps in the home may help. Light therapy may also be an option.

Light therapy involves sitting under lights that are up to ten times brighter than usual for up to two hours a day. If there is no improvement within a week, longer periods of therapy may be required. The therapy also needs to be continuous during the winter months, because symptoms often return when it is stopped.

Depending on your economic situation, a holiday in the sun or even relocating to a warmer climate are options.

Suggesting that he doesn't undertake big life-changing events (such as moving house or starting a new job) during the winter months is helpful. He should also watch his caffeine intake, as some nutritionists believe that too much caffeine aggravates symptoms of SAD.

Sleep

Getting the right amount of sleep will significantly reduce anxiety and stress. Both lack of sleep and too much sleep can make a man feel tired, stressed and out of condition. Most of us need around eight hours of sleep a night to function well. Without adequate sleep we quickly become depressed, irritated and fuzzy-headed.

When a man is feeling anxious, his sleep patterns may be disrupted. He may wake early in the morning or may find it hard to get to sleep at all. Research has shown that depressed people get less deep sleep, which is the most restorative and refreshing. So even if they sleep for many hours, they still feel exhausted when they wake up.

Sleep disruption is a sign that the man you care about has a biological clock that is out of kilter. Getting the right amount of sleep may significantly reduce his anxiety and stress. Strategies you might want to suggest to help regulate his sleep patterns include:

- a quick biological clock reset: Dr Mark S Gold of the University of Florida Medical School suggests staying awake for 24 hours. In many cases this seems to reset a biological clock that is out of kilter, for the short term if not the long term.
- taking a dose of carefully regulated melatonin
- shifting his bedtime to five or six hours earlier, then gradually moving it back to its usual time
- going to bed and getting up at the same time each day
- following the same food schedule each day
- avoiding caffeine, alcohol and drugs
- learning relaxation techniques if he tends to wake in the middle of the night or too early in the morning.

Let's Talk About Sex

When a man is feeling blue, sex may improve his mood, but more commonly there may be a loss of libido, especially if the depression is severe.

If you are his partner and the two of you have been having sex regularly, be it once a week or once a month, and sex suddenly drops off for no apparent reason, you may be suspicious. It's hard not to feel rejected, but just because a man doesn't want to have sex so often doesn't mean he doesn't love you anymore or is having an affair. A sex life that has gone stale could be a contributory factor, but there are lots of other reasons why a man goes off sex or fails to get an erection – drinking to excess, weight problems, poor health, diabetes, poor blood flow in the lower body and, perhaps, the most common reasons – depression and worry.

Age shouldn't be a factor. Men over 50 may want sex less often, but sex should continue to give them pleasure and there is no reason why they shouldn't enjoy an active sex life. If you have been together for a long time, and you have many demands or responsibilities, like work or children, a diminution in desire is understandable. But if you talk to your partner and he claims that he isn't interested in sex anymore, don't accept this at face value. Asexuality is complex, and there may not be such a thing as a person not liking sex. A disinterest in sex usually covers up an aversion or fear of sex and intimacy. It can stem from fear of being controlled, suppressed anger, or a fear of expressing emotions.

Loss of libido can be devastating and humiliating to a man's self-esteem. He may welcome you initiating sex, but he may also resent it if you take the initiative and he can't get aroused. It's worth talking this over together, remembering that the situation needs to be handled very sensitively. Somehow you need to convey to him that the very fact you are missing regular sex is not a criticism but a good sign and it should give him confidence in the relationship.

If you find this too difficult to discuss without professional help, it might be worth finding a qualified sex therapist or counsellor to help you communicate more honestly and openly about sex. Help for a wide variety of problems is offered at all Relate (Marriage Guidance) offices throughout the UK, and a growing number of specialized counsellors in both the US and the UK offer sex therapy.

If the sexual disinterest has been long term, it could be linked to emotional trauma or sexual abuse. Your partner may not even be aware of the connection between his emotional wounds and his aversion to sex. If he has experienced this kind of trauma, and it still distresses him, encourage him to get help.

Erection Problems

Generally speaking, if the man you care about gets an erection on waking or at certain other times, there is unlikely to be a physical cause for erection problems. You could try asking him what arousal techniques will be helpful. If, however, he consistently fails to get an erection he should see a doctor to exclude factors such as diabetes, poor blood flow, side-effects of medication or alcohol, as well as serious anxiety or depression.

Aids to impotence include self-injection with a drug that causes erection. Not all men cope well with this – it takes time to overcome natural fears – but it can work. Another simple aid is a rubber ring placed around the base of the penis. And of course there's Viagra, which looks set to transform the treatment of impotence. Viagra needs to be taken an hour before intercourse, and its main side-effect seems to be a headache.

Should erection problems be causing or adding to a man's depression, he and you might benefit from professional relationship counselling. Communication, here again, will be key.

Coming Out

Surveys suggest that up to 5 per cent of men have experienced gay sex. An even higher percentage – up to 25 per cent – experience some attraction towards other men, though this may only be a temporary phase during adolescence. Men who identify themselves as gay find that sexual contact with men is preferable to sexual contact with women.

If a man feels powerfully attracted to another man, he may experience feelings of shame, guilt and anxiety, reflecting a conflict between the way his upbringing is pushing him and the way his emotions are pulling him. In recent times there has been much greater tolerance of gay relationships, although coming out can still be a source of anxiety for some men if they do not have the support of friends or family. The London Lesbian and Gay Switchboard (see Resources chapter) can offer advice.

Helping Him Cope with Stress and Anxiety

Stress isn't necessarily bad, so don't encourage the man you care about to avoid stress altogether. He needs a little stress to provide him with motivation and to challenge him. Positive stress offers him healthy stimulation, and his life would be dull without it. Problems only arise when stress levels exceed his ability to cope and begin to affect him negatively. He needs to learn how to manage his stress, not banish it all together.

Anxiety means worry that is mingled with fear. A man's mind roves over the possible ways that things could go wrong. When a man is anxious he often can't concentrate, he seems on edge and irritable most of the time, he may lose his libido, and in some cases he may not be able to function at all. There may be headaches, aching muscles, and a dry mouth and stomach upsets. Anxiety often overlaps with stress, and if the mental rumination is unchecked, it can lead to depression.

Some men are naturally anxious and worry all their lives. Other men become worriers because of stresses placed upon them by themselves or others. Tolerance of stress varies from man to man. Some men go on taking risks and thrive on stress. Others don't cope so well. Much also depends on the nature of the stress and the circumstances of the man's life at the time.

You can recognize particular stress triggers when a man is more vulnerable. These triggers are usually about loss of control, something most men fear terribly. They fall into four categories: work and money, temperament and health, relationships, and lifestyle.

If you recognize that a man seems to have lost control in some area of his life, the first step he needs to take is to identify his stress trigger. Then you might suggest that he draw up an action plan (a few brief examples are given below), with the aim of regaining control over his life.

Debt	**Talk to the bank manager about refinancing debt. If more than one person or organization is owed money, it's cheaper to organize a single loan to pay them all off.**
Low salary	**Make sure of the going rate for any kind of work. Then negotiate a pay rise, but with the understanding that this will take time and effort.**
Unreasonable boss	**Consider the possibility of making a complaint, transferring to another department or job, or hiring extra help to take the pressure off.**
Stressful travelling and long hours	**Investigate alternative means of getting to work. Investigate changing jobs. Investigate the possibility of working from home.**
Unemployment	**Not having a job is not a social disaster and not something to be ashamed off. It's another phase in a person's career. Improve skill base and start applying for jobs.**
Constant worrying	**Try to gain a sense of perspective, and to tackle each source of worry in turn.**
Quick temper or impatience	**Take deep breaths or count to ten. Losing one's temper can send blood pressure racing.**

Poor health	Draw up an action plan for coping. Learn about the condition. Perhaps join a support group.
Divorce	Don't hide feelings from friends and family. If it all gets to feel too much, seek some kind of support group or professional counselling.
Becoming a father	Keep the lines of communication open with partner, and remember that the birth of a child is a stressful event for her, too.
Bereavement	Don't be too proud to accept offers of help during this traumatic time. Stay in touch with those who care. Seek out a support group or professional counsellor or therapist.
Moving house	Try to break the task down into manageable chunks, and get help from friends and family with practical details.
Information Overload	Take time out to re-charge the batteries.

RELAXATION AND STRESS-REDUCTION TECHNIQUES

Regular exercise, a healthy diet, decent sleep, taking time out for himself and interacting with others all contribute to relaxation, but there's also a range of relaxation techniques which can be employed to overcome the negative effects of stress and anxiety. Discuss what would suit him and encourage him to include it in his routine. Many of the techniques recommended for you in Chapter 5 can also help him, and you might like to do them together.

If he is reluctant to engage in any relaxation techniques, even if he tries nothing else suggest that he masters the technique of breathing in a way intended to reduce stress. The technique of breathing in and out deeply and evenly can be employed at any time and in any place, whenever anxiety or feelings of hopelessness threaten to overwhelm him.

Helping Him When He Hits a Life Crisis

The man you care about may get the blues when he hits a life crisis. He may lose his job, get mugged, he may find that his partner is having an affair and so on. It might seem obvious what the problem is, but there may be other, more complicated emotional issues beneath the surface. Understanding the myriad ways he might be affected will help you support him through the crisis.

LOSING SOMEONE

When someone dies or leaves, you might expect grief and tears from the man you care about. What you get may be far more complicated. He may go into denial that the person has left him. He may blame himself for the loss. He may be furious. And this may go on, not just for weeks, but for months. If this is so, and he feels that talking about his loss will help, bereavement counselling is available (see Resources chapter).

You need to be a gentle support for as long as it takes. Allow him to move from mood to mood. Listen to what he has to say. The stages of grief are perfectly natural, yet can take much longer than most people think.

WHEN HE IS ILL OR INJURED

When a man gets ill or injured, not only will he be feeling weak, ghastly and exhausted, but worries may crowd his mind, too. He may panic that he is never going to get better. He may worry that he can't pay the bills. He may lose his confidence if he has had an accident. He may start to review his life and feel unhappy with it.

If you want to support a man who is feeling down when he is ill, offer practical help but also encourage him to explore his feelings with a counsellor to help him to feel in control again.

IF HE IS MUGGED OR BURGLED

When a man is robbed he will feel angry and upset, but he will also feel violated and exposed. It may take weeks, months or even years for him to come to terms with the situation and the fear that it will happen again.

If you want to support him, bear in mind that being robbed is not just about the loss of material possessions; it's all about his space being invaded and his trust being betrayed. Help him explore these feelings so that he understands that one person or group of persons did this to him, not everyone he encounters.

IF HE DISCOVERS HIS PARTNER HAS BEEN UNFAITHFUL

He feels betrayed, rejected, angry, sad and unloved. He has also lost his faith and trust in other people. The key here is to avoid any hint of blame for either party; just listen, accept, and support him. Let him know that someone is there for him and he can begin to build up trust in other people again.

Work Issues

Work issues like redundancy, promotion or retirement are never just about money. They are about perceptions of failing, or how society values you. Even success can cause a man concern. He may worry that he is not up to the job or that he will be exposed as a failure. When suffering work strain, a man needs to regain lost confidence. He can do this better, not by being told he is a success, but by being supported so that he comes to believe he is a success. You can encourage him to work out what he needs to succeed.

Coping with change is never easy, but change is a fact of life. You might remind him of that and suggest that he gets involved in planning for change, considers retraining, asking for feedback on his career from others. Encourage him to keep a sense of humour and perspective. No one in business or work is ever indispensable, and there is great wisdom in the cliché that no man on his deathbed wishes he had spent more time at the office.

Workaholism and Burnout

Men often expect themselves to get on with things, regardless of the pressures. They often ignore physical or emotional symptoms longer than women might, resist other people's emotional demands, not say how they feel, and definitely not cry.

Given these habits, is it any surprise that men are prone to workaholism and burnout?

The workaholic man allows his work to take priority over everything in his life, including his family, friends and his health, and if the situation is not remedied it soon gets out of hand. He may also be in danger of burnout when his physical and emotional health suffer because of the pressure and long hours and he can't motivate himself anymore. If a man you know is a workaholic or suffering from burnout, how can you help him?

You can encourage him to think about what work means to him, what he enjoys and what he doesn't. Suggest that he considers whether or not the job can be adjusted to make it more suitable. Perhaps he could review his working week and cut down on the number of hours, shed some responsibility or get things in perspective by taking a holiday or a sabbatical. Above all, encourage him to develop hobbies or interests outside of work so that work does not become the sole source of his satisfaction. If this fails, he may have to consider changing his job or altering his life altogether.

Parents

If he is feeling down because he has parent problems, prepare for unexpected reactions. The relationship between parent and child starts out as one of complete dependence. If a parent dies or has an illness or is in money trouble, a man may suddenly go to pieces, whatever age he is. He may suddenly feel very lonely, unprotected, young and vulnerable in a big, scary world. Or he may feel suddenly free and empowered, and this can cause feelings of guilt. Your role again is to listen and support and to remind yourself that when a parent dies the man you care about is likely to see life in a different way.

Helping Him Cope with Midlife Changes

Physiological changes at midlife and a decline in testosterone can trigger a diminished sex drive, decreased bone density, depression and fatigue in some men.

Dr Carruthers, author of *Maximizing Manhood: Beating the Male Menopause*, advises stress-reduction, regular exercise, mental stimulation, avoiding alcohol and ensuring a healthy diet as ways to ease the symptoms. He also suggests hormone replacement therapy for declining levels of testosterone.

A testosterone gel that is rubbed onto the shoulders to boost testosterone levels could soon be available. In clinical trials this colourless, odourless hormone-replacement gel substantially increased testosterone levels in the blood of more than 200 men under the age of 68.

The midlife drop in testosterone is something most men are reluctant to acknowledge and discuss. You need to be sensitive to that. Suggest that he read Carruthers' books or other similar books, or talk to his doctor. If he is considering HRT, he needs to discuss all the available options with his doctor. Testosterone therapy for men is still an area of great controversy.

Psychological changes taking place at midlife may cause a man to feel that he is sinking in quicksand. The more he struggles, the more he sinks. He may respond with indifference to outside help, but he does need your help and support even if you give that help in indirect ways.

If you are his employer, recognize that this is a short-term crisis and that he can continue to be a productive employee and probably more valuable in the long term because he has a wider perspective.

If you are his friend, you need to understand that life is a series of developmental changes. Even though he may give you a lot of abuse, your task is to not give up on him and continue to care. Remember, genuine friendship requires unqualified acceptance of both the good and bad in a person.

If you are the child of a man in midlife crisis, don't withdraw or treat him as though he has leprosy. Remind him how much you appreciate him, and mention things to build his self-esteem.

If you are his partner, nurture the powerful connection you've build up. Understand his problem as a stage in his life he needs to experience. Find ways of gently bringing him out of his cage of withdrawal by building his self-esteem, reminding him of what he does well, and encouraging him in new areas of growth.

Helping a Man Discover What He Needs to Feel Happy

According to Steve Biddulph, author of *Raising Boys* and *Manhood*, boys need to experience certain rites of passage in order to become men. It's possible that if a man hasn't met his developmental needs adequately, this may explain feelings of sadness, disappointment and inadequacy that seem to have no justifiable cause.

There is no one cure for the male blues, but perhaps you could encourage the man you care about to consider the possibility that the following might promote his happiness as a man.

1   THINKING ABOUT HIS RELATIONSHIP WITH HIS FATHER

A man's father is his model for masculinity. It's hard for a man to get on with his own life if he hasn't understood his father, forgiven him, and in some way come to respect him. He can do this while his father is alive or, in his mind, even if his father is dead. If his relationship with his father is non-existent or intolerable, a man needs to learn to respect the father potential within himself (see point 4, below).

2   CELEBRATING HIS SEXUALITY

Many men think about sex a lot, but many don't actually find it as fulfilling as they'd hoped. Finding out how to be comfortable and fulfilled in his sexuality can be a source of well-being. He needs to locate the source of his sexual power within himself rather than projecting it onto other women or men.

3   MEETING A PARTNER ON EQUAL TERMS

A man needs to learn to treat his partner, or the people that are special in his life, as different but equal beings. That means respecting himself and respecting others. It means learning to communicate so that a balance between his needs and those of others is achieved.

4   FULFILLING HIS FATHER POTENTIAL

If a man has children, he has to take an active part in the parenting of his children. Children depend on their fathers for a large slice of their self-esteem. They need his time and active participation in their upbringing. If a man decides not to have children or can't have children, he needs to find other ways to nurture. He can nurture other people, other people's children, animals, projects at work, projects in the community, and so on. There are many ways to father, apart from the biological.

5 LEARNING TO HAVE MALE FRIENDS

One way for a man to find out how to complete his initiation into manhood is to get emotional support from other men. All men need the help of other men at certain key moments in their lives.

6 FINDING WORK THAT FULFILS HIM

A man needs to find work that fulfils him so that he isn't just making a living. He needs to feel that he is supporting and protecting life and building towards a better world. Not believing in the work that he does can make a man feel empty and contradicted.

7 FINDING A SPIRITUAL BASIS

A man needs to find a spiritual basis for his life that isn't based on material achievements. He needs to find an inner life that reconnects him with nature, frees him from dependency on others, and acts as a source of strength and harmony.

Having faith can reduce stress and depression. Depending on your belief systems, you may want to pray together. Researchers at Duke University Medical Center in Durham, North Carolina, found that people who attended religious services had stronger immune systems. This might be due to the stress-reducing powers of social contact, but it is possible that prayer itself can relax us. It seems that turning to another source or simply envisioning greater happiness for themselves can help men feel more in control of their lives.

Biddulph believes that all these steps are vital if a man is to develop to full manhood. The issue here is not whether or not you and the man you care about agree with Biddulph. The important thing is to contemplate the points raised to encourage him to really think about what he needs in his life to be happy, fulfilled and contented and to change his life for the better.

The activities and ideas suggested in this chapter can help considerably when a man is feeling blue or mildly depressed. If, however, the man you care about continues to ruminate on negative thoughts, is immune to your help and support, and seems to be spiralling ever further into depression, he may need outside help.

How to recognize when a man's depression needs treatment, and how to encourage him to seek treatment, will be explored in the next chapter.

8

Helping Him Seek Help

I was further out than you thought
and not waving but drowning.

Stevie Smith

The help *you* can provide is needed when a man is feeling blue, or at the onset of mild depression. If symptoms progress, however, and the man you care about finds his motivation eroding, he will lose his ability to help himself and respond to suggestions that might make him feel better. He can't see why he should bother, he's bound to get worse. When a man is no longer able to take action to improve his mood, outside help needs to be brought in.

Recognizing that He Needs Outside Help

If the man you care about is reluctant to tackle work, avoids social gatherings, refuses to make an effort to feel better, and lessens his involvement in leisurely pursuits, he needs professional help. Also, if you notice four or more of the following symptoms for more than two weeks, the man you care about is severely depressed. Outside help is no longer an option; it is essential:

- He feels hopeless, helpless and inadequate.
- He dislikes himself and has a constant need for reassurance.
- He seems oversensitive and vulnerable.
- He is violent, abusive or harming himself.
- He has lost or gained a lot of weight.
- He is having problems sleeping or he is sleeping too much.
- He has lost his sex drive.
- He can't concentrate and is forgetful.
- He has a sense of unreality.
- He has mysterious aches and pains and fears something bad will happen to him.

Treatment for depression has a very high success rate: 90 per cent of those suffering can find relief quickly, and the remaining 10 per cent find longer-term relief. It's good to know this, because you may be feeling anxious and uncertain about the benefits of treatment.

Modern treatments for depression can and do work. The situation is not hopeless. The big problem is that when men are depressed, their sense of hopelessness makes it difficult for them to reach out. According to the US National Institute of Mental Health, only a third of those needing treatment for depression actually receive it. Your challenge now is to encourage him to seek the help he desperately needs.

You probably have many questions: How can I get him to seek treatment? What treatment is best? What about side-effects? What can I expect? How long till he gets better? and so on. Hopefully this chapter will help you answer all these questions and show you how you can support him in seeking and maintaining a treatment programme that is right for him.

Encouraging Him to Seek Treatment

When you become sure that outside help is needed, more often than not the man you care about also knows this is true. But what if he has still said nothing? How do you suggest he seeks help?

You suggest it very gently.

Don't let him think you are abandoning him, criticizing him or that you think he is beyond hope. Instead, tell him you are concerned about him and want to find a way to help him. Don't let him think he has no say in what's happening. Make it clear that bringing in outside help is a suggestion only, and that if he chooses outside help he won't lose your support.

But what if you have been ever so tactful and he still refuses to seek help? Then he has a right not to do so; it's his issue. Women especially tend to feel responsible for the health of their husbands and family but, unless he is under 18, the only person who is responsible for his health is him.

You can't force him to the doctors against his will. It may be clear to you that he is depressed, but he has to reach his own understanding in his own time. There are exceptions to this rule, and later we'll discuss what to do in when a man seems to have lost all control, but if this isn't the case all you can do is continue to accept him and offer your support if he wants it.

The chances are he is refusing support because he has many fears. Here are a few common ones:

He may be afraid of the unknown.
If this is the case, offer to get lots of information for him about what treatment for depression involves.
He may think he can't afford treatment.
You could find out about low-cost options for what he needs.
He may be terrified that his diagnosis will be bad.
You can offer to be there for him whatever his diagnosis is.
He may be so depressed he can't cope with arranging anything new.
You could offer to do the practicalities, phone to arrange appointments, drive him to the doctor and so on.

He may be scared of being judged as 'bad' or 'mad' or 'dangerous'.
You could let him know you accept him however negative he feels.
He may be afraid of losing control when outside help comes in.
If this is the case, offer to be with him when the experts are around.
*He may be scared that a doctor will be shocked or bored by his
problems.*
Reassure him that most doctors and counsellors are very hard to shock
and are very accepting.

Helping him seek help can be the most important thing you do
for him. Here are a few ways you can encourage him to take
that important step:

- Find out as much as possible about depression before talking about
  it to him. The better informed you are, the better the chance he
  will accept the information you offer.
- Leave information and leaflets lying around for him to look at.
- Encourage him to use a telephone helpline; many men prefer to
  speak about their problems anonymously.
- Offer to go with him to his doctor or even make an appointment
  on his behalf, which he has the option to cancel.

Finding Help for the Man You Care About, Whatever Your Relationship with Him

In finding help for the depressed man in your life, much
depends on your relationship with him.

Your Child

Recognizing that your child is depressed in the first place is the
hardest challenge. Symptoms of depression in children are
often masked in perfectly normal developmental behaviour like
tantrums and anxiety.

Six-year-old Stuart was showing signs of depression after the birth of his sister. Stuart became clingy and whiny, but sometimes there would be uncharacteristically violent outbursts of aggression. His mother was asked to withdraw him from school when he started biting other children. 'He's biting to get attention,' his mother complained.

Often it's hard to accept that your child may be depressed.

Also, if your child has dyslexia, attention deficit disorder, learning difficulties or other special needs, the frustrations they create may manifest as depression.

If you suspect that your child may be depressed, the first step is to rule out any physical disorder. A physical examination undertaken by your doctor will achieve this. If there are no physical problems, the next step is for your doctor to refer him for psychological treatment.

Some doctors may recommend that you review your child's diet. There is a link between depression, anxiety, poor concentration and hyperactivity with a diet high in sugars and fat and junk food. Studies show that when children cut back on sweets and fizzy drinks and eat a diet high in nutrients, behaviour often shows a marked improvement.

Things get more complicated when your son is no longer a child but a teenager. If you push him towards help, he is likely to rebel. He may feel ashamed of being different or resent you interfering with his newfound independence.

Watch out for symptoms of depression which go on for more than two weeks and which interfere with normal functioning. Consider carefully if the difficulties you are having are nothing more than typical teenage rebellion or if there is something deeper. Ask yourself:

Is he losing interest in activities he normally enjoyed?
Does he often seem close to tears?
Is he angry or impatient with you?
Has his behaviour changed – either more withdrawn or unusually animated?

Is his self-esteem low?
Does he have low energy and difficulty concentrating?
Is he sleeping too much or too little?
Is he eating too much or too little?
Are there signs that he may be taking drugs or drinking too much alcohol?
Are you afraid of him?

Talk to other parents to find out how they are coping with their children. Talk to his teachers at school to asses his behaviour. If they will let you, talk to his peers at school or college. If you are still in doubt, listen to your intuition. As far as teenage boys are concerned, it is better to be cautious.

Trust your instincts: If you are concerned, you're probably right. Encourage him to seek emotional support, and set aside time to listen to him without offering advice or opinions – something many parents find very hard to do. If he is feeling sad, empty and worthless, tell him that he may need help. He'll probably tell you that you don't understand. Don't tell him that you do understand, that you were a teenager once, that it was different in your day. Instead, tell him that he is probably right. You don't understand, so that's why you want to get help. When you approach him in this accepting, non-judgemental way, you may just find that he is willing to participate.

If your son is starting college or university and you are worried, find out what psychological health services are available there. Point out over and over again that depression is treatable. Make sure that if he won't talk to you, he knows there is someone else to consult. Most universities offer confidential support services. *Nightline* in the UK says many young men suffer from 'small fish, big pond' syndrome when they arrive fresh from cozy homes and schools where they were academic high achievers to discover they are surrounded by equally bright peers. There is often an underlying feeling of isolation and a sense of not being able to cope, and a fear of admitting to that which leads to low self-esteem.

If he is still reluctant, you may need to talk to a doctor or mental health specialist about the next step. Some experts believe that if nothing else works and if physical exams rule out any other disorder, you should force depressed teenage boys to receive treatment, hospitalize them or place them in treatment programmes for their own good. This is especially the case if alcohol and/or drugs and violence are concerned. But before you consider that, you might want to try the kind of approach you would use if your child were an adult.

If your adult child is depressed, you could enlist the support of other family members, his partner (if he has one) and his friends. The relationship between parent and child is often too subjective, and other people may be able to be more objective and reach him better than you can.

Your adult son may find it hard to acknowledge that he is depressed, especially to you. You may find it hard not to become overly involved. Remember, though, that the only way he is going to recover is to take responsibility for his depression. Your challenge is to communicate your concern in a way that respects his independence but that also lets him know you accept him and support him. Something like: 'You seem to be unhappy. I know you can take care of yourself, but is there is anything I can do to help right now?'

Your focus must be on how to help your son, not how to take charge of him. If he still won't seek help, enlist the support of his friends, his partner, his coworkers or people you know he trusts. The danger here is that he will take offence at your interference, so make sure you are sensitive and know when to back off. If he is over 30, the dynamic of your relationship will change again. You can't parent him anymore. You must respect his independence. All you can do is offer him your concern and your support.

Your Friend

If a friend of yours is depressed, your relationship will be similar to that of an adult child. You show your concern and your support, but you respect his independence. Accept that you can't have as much control as you would like and that you can't force him to seek help. You could try to get his family members, other friends and his partner involved, but your helping stops there. If you are having trouble knowing how to cope with his depression, you might benefit from some outside support yourself.

Your Father

It is often the case that when parents stop parenting us, we start parenting them. Depending on the severity of his depression and the degree of closeness between you and your father (or even your grandfather), you may be called upon to take charge of his condition and his treatment. This time you may have more control than you would like, and you need to be clear in your own mind about how much responsibility you are going to take and how caring for him fits into your life.

If he is reluctant to seek treatment and insists that he doesn't want to be a burden, you might want to enlist the help of other family members and your doctor. Make it clear to him that you love him and will take whatever action you think is necessary to help him, even if that means organizing a hospital evaluation.

Many physical conditions associated with getting older, and many medications used, can trigger or mimic depression, so if your father is depressed or seems forgetful and confused, a physical examination should be undertaken to rule out other conditions first. If no physical cause is found, his doctor will refer him to a mental health specialist.

Doctors can often tell the difference between depression and another condition, like dementia, by asking questions of fact such as, 'Where do you live?' or 'What is your date of birth?' Depressed men give half-hearted, vague answers and may even say they don't know or can't remember, but they will make some kind of effort to answer the question. Those with dementia will give a grossly inaccurate reply, indicating that they haven't understood the question.

Your Partner

When I suggested to my boyfriend that he needed help, he slammed his fist down on a glass table and broke it in anger.

You care for someone and you want them to feel better. Your partner may respond to your concern and co-operate, but he may also see your concern as an insult.

Trying to get a reluctant partner, husband or boyfriend to see a doctor can seem an insurmountable obstacle. Fearing that you may humiliate or insult him, you may stop insisting that he seek much-needed treatment.

There are ways you can encourage a reluctant partner to co-operate. Much depends on the severity of his depression and the strength of the bonds between you. First of all, make it clear that you are encouraging him to seek help and are withstanding his protests because you love and care for him. The next step is to seek advice from your doctor or another health professional. Ensure also that family, friends and those you can trust are able to give you their support.

When you are sure you have enough inner conviction and outside support, you can develop a plan of action. Hopefully this plan will be developed with the man you care about and your doctor. If he still won't co-operate, tell him that if he doesn't want to work with you on a voluntary basis you are prepared to inform a hospital or a doctor that he needs treatment. You will do what is necessary to make him seek help.

You may well find that following such a plan has the desired effect.

Angie was concerned about her husband, Tony. After his father died, Tony's mood began to deteriorate. Angie watched him change from an outgoing, positive, energetic man into one who didn't even have the energy to pick up the phone. She urged him to see a doctor, but Tony just told her he needed time to grieve.

Angie sensed that something was deeply wrong. She knew that, whatever it took, Tony needed help. She talked to Tony's mother and sister and explained the situation. She asked them if they were prepared to help her take him to see a doctor. With the family supporting her, Angie told Tony how worried about him she was and that it might be wise for him to see a doctor. To her amazement, Tony agreed. He phoned the doctor there and then.

Throughout his treatment, Angie remained by his side, reassuring him of her love and support. At times it wasn't easy for either of them, and Angie turned to a therapist to support her through the crisis.

Angie's emotional resolve was the catalyst for change here. Once you believe that the man you care about needs help and that help can make him feel better, you may just find that he stops challenging you and is relieved to co-operate with you. Equally crucial is the support of others and the support you give yourself. Sometimes if enough people tell a man that they care about him, but that he needs expert guidance to get better, the message gets through. And sometimes when the going gets tough you need to accept that *you* might need help and support from others, too.

Where to Go First?

You know that bringing in outside support is the right thing to do, but you aren't sure where to start. You may wonder where you should go to seek advice and help, and what kind of help is available.

Your Local Health Centre or Doctor's Surgery

Doctors are likely to be the first port of call for you to get advice, and for the man you care about to get a physical examination to rule out any other conditions that might be causing his mood disorder.

A doctor will want the man you care about to tell him or her how he feels in detail, whether any triggers might explain his mood, whether he is drinking a lot, and whether he has thoughts of suicide. A mental health assessment will also be made. He may be asked if there is a family history of depression or if he is on any current medication. All this is important in confirming the diagnosis and deciding the type and urgency of treatment, and whether or not the man you care about needs to be referred to a mental health professional.

Sometimes a man may find it helpful simply to have it explained to him by his doctor that the symptoms he has add up to depression. For milder cases this may be all that he needs, other than counselling and therapy.

A man's doctor is his link to a wide variety of support services. Through his doctor he may be able to get counselling on the NHS if you live in the UK, practical help such as meals on wheels, or other support services. You can find doctors listed in the phone book, or through directory inquiries. In an emergency call 999 in the UK, 911 or your local police in the US, or go to a hospital's casualty department.

Citizens' Advice Bureaux (UK)

The Citizens' Advice Bureau will help with practical (but not medical) problems. This is where you can get free, impartial and confidential information or advice on subjects ranging from divorce, employment, law, discrimination, debt and so on. You can find your nearest Citizens' Advice Bureau in the Yellow Pages.

Human Resources or Personnel Officer

If the man you are helping has work-related problems or if his depression is affecting his job, the Human Resources Department or Personnel Office where he works may be a helpful resource. Ask for confidentiality if you think that acknowledging problems will affect his job prospects. The Personnel Officer should be able to help with friction at work or, if the problem is outside work, to suggest the next step to take. If the man you are helping doesn't have a Personnel Officer or is out of work, the Citizens' Advice Bureau, local libraries or information centres may be able to advise.

Turning to a Higher Source

You or the man you care about may not be religious, but many people turn to spirituality for comfort in times of trouble. Talking through the possibilities with members of a person's faith, if he has one, may help. They may also be able to give practical, day-to-day assistance. Your phone directory or local newspaper will have details of local places of worship.

Telephone Helplines

If you want support instantly, a telephone helpline is a good option. This sort of support is often linked to a particular crisis, illness or issue, and many of the helplines are run by charities or major national organizations.

Not all helplines are satisfactory, so be careful. Make sure they aren't charging for the call, and that all calls are confidential. The phone helpers should also be fully trained in offering the correct kind of emotional support and suggesting further treatment. Your local library should have a Telephone Helpers Directory which lists those with trained and qualified staff in your state or country. In the UK, find out if the helpline is a member of the Telephone Helplines Association – an organization that encourages good practice (see Resources chapter, where there is also a list of useful helpline numbers).

If you think you have found the right helpline, give him the number and encourage him to call. If he does make a call, you might want to be there after the call so that he can discuss with you how it made him feel.

One of the most well-known helplines in the UK is the Samaritans. If you think mentioning the Samaritans to him might signal that you think he is suicidal, try to make him aware that the Samaritans are not just for moments of utter despair; the Samaritans are also there for anyone who needs to talk about how they are feeling in a safe and confidential manner. In fact, the Samaritans prefer it if callers contact them *before* feelings threaten to overwhelm them. Nothing is too trivial to the Samaritans, so do make a point of suggesting that he call them – or call them yourself on his behalf. Samaritans will then discreetly contact him, if that is appropriate, and offer support. Other crisis lines with trained staff operate along similar guidelines.

If a man has never called a crisis line before, he may wonder what to expect. The answer is that when he calls, a person will say 'hello' and ask how he or she can help. That person will then listen to what the man you care about has to say. They won't judge, criticize or give advice, and the conversation is in complete confidence. The listener will simply allow a man to explore how he feels.

Support Groups

Support groups meet regularly, often locally and often in halls or houses. They are formed around the experience of depression, illness or addiction and offer every member of the group a chance to share their experience. Talking to others can be reassuring and comforting. Support is given and support is received, and members feel less of a sense of isolation as a result.

If the man you are helping wants to meet others who are feeling the same way, lists of support groups can be found at doctors' practices or health centres. Many of the organizations listed in the Resources chapter also run support groups, and you might want to phone them for details. Your library, health centre or hospital may also have a list of self-help support groups in your area.

Although you may find that local support groups for the family and friends of depressed people are a comfort to you, the man you care about may be reluctant to join a support group for depressed people. He may have preconceived notions about what joining a support group might mean, or he may be reluctant because of long-held fears. He might fear feeling awkward and inhibited. He may fear that he will be pressured by the group. He may feel that he has to try what works for someone else. He may be afraid that he will feel inadequate if others feel better and he doesn't.

If he does join a group, he may worry that getting better will cut him off from the support of the group. If he has found a sense of community in the group, getting better will remove him from that base of support. If the man you care about has joined a support group and you or he has concerns about the group, he may wish to talk to you first about these concerns.

Self-help Information Gathering

Books, magazines, TV programmes, video, the internet and leaflets are terrific sources of information. If the man you care about doesn't enjoy reading, perhaps you could relay the information to him. Many of the organizations listed in the Resources chapter provide information or recommend books. Usually this is free, although sometimes a SAE and a small fee are required. Your library should have a list of voluntary agencies in your state or country.

In the US, you are fortunate to have a number of excellent information centres, research institutes and consumer advocacy groups dedicated to understanding and treating depression. Some, but by no means all, are listed in the Resources chapter.

In the UK, the National Association for Mental Health (MIND) offers nationwide support for anyone worried about their own or another's mental health.

Selected books are listed in the Resources chapter, but you can get lots of good information under the medical, health, self-help, psychology, men's issues and popular psychology sections in your local bookshop or library.

The internet is a vast maze of information, some of it incredibly good, some of it downright inaccurate and written by non-experts. Don't rely on it as an accurate source of information at all times. The Resources chapter lists internet sites provided by various support organizations that you can trust.

Hopefully this chapter has helped you encourage the man you care about to seek advice, preferably from his doctor. If treatment is required, the treatment should have as its goal an abatement of symptoms, a return to normal functioning, and the prevention of a relapse, but a treatment can work only if a man is prepared to participate in it. In Chapter 10 we'll look at what you can expect from the medical profession. We'll also explore what to do if, despite your support and encouragement, the man you care about still refuses treatment.

But before that, it is important to discuss the most terrible outcome of depression: suicide. Sometimes gently encouraging a man to see a doctor isn't the right approach. You need to be able to recognize when urgent action is necessary, and to know what to do when it is.

9

Is He in Danger?

When a man attempts suicide, those who care about him feel intense grief and shock. There is also guilt:

'I should have seen this coming.'
'There must have been something I could have done to stop him.'
'Why didn't I notice the warning signs?'
'This didn't need to happen.'

Many relatives and friends of depressed men who attempt suicide have little or no idea what he is going through – and spend the rest of their lives regretting that they had no chance to help him. Parents, partners and family members are sometimes the last to know what is really going on inside a man's mind.

It's frightening to hear that a man you care about may wish to do the unthinkable, so you may not want to raise the subject or even think about it. Those who are not quite so emotionally involved, like friends and teachers, may have a feeling that something is wrong, but even they may not imagine there might be such a terrible outcome.

Tom killed himself after the increasingly bleak future of farming became too much to bear. His family had run a farm for generations, but a month after his 55th birthday Tom, who was battling depression, felt there was no point in carrying on. He went for a walk and never returned. His body

was found hanging in the cowshed. His wife, Sheila, had noticed that he seemed more argumentative and moody, but she put it down to the financial problems. His farming colleagues worried that Tom seemed overwhelmingly negative about the future, and his grandson, Eric, was disturbed by his grandfather's obsession with death, but no one thought he would take things that far.

You may fear that asking the man you care about if he is thinking about taking his own life may make it happen. But asking about it is more likely to do the opposite. Talking about what he is planning may release him from desperate thoughts and allow him to think about other options.

But how do you ask a man if he is thinking about suicide?

It's probably best to begin gently, asking him if he feels worse than usual or if he feels life isn't worth living, or if he ever thinks about harming himself. If he says he is not thinking about suicide and you are still worried, remain aware. If he does say that he is thinking about suicide, get as much support from family and friends as you can, and try to encourage him to seek help and treatment.

Unfortunately, sometimes there just aren't any warning signs, but in many cases there are. Even if you ultimately can't prevent him acting, though nothing can ever take away the pain of his loss, knowing that you did everything you possibly could may offer some kind of solace.

Risk Factors

First of all, let's outline certain circumstances that put a man more at risk of suicide:

- A history of depression, mental illness, abuse in childhood, or previous suicide attempts increases risk.

- Men who are single and childless have a higher risk, closely followed by men who are widowed, separated or divorced. Married men with no children and married men with children follow in order of risk.
- A man who has a major work crisis such as job loss, unemployment or bankruptcy is at higher risk.
- If a man is over 65 he is 15 times more likely to attempt suicide, according to Dr Mark S Gold of the University of Florida Medical School.
- If a man is in chronic physical pain or has a terminal illness, his risk is higher.
- If a man is addicted to alcohol, drugs or other substances, his risk is higher.
- When a man appears to be getting better, this is, perhaps surprisingly, a time of high risk. The apathy of depression will have lifted, but the suicidal thoughts remain and he has more energy to take action.
- When depression is coupled with intense anxiety and panic attacks, risk increases considerably.
- Starting or leaving college or university can be a time of high risk for some young men. When they enter a new environment they are less sheltered from the knocks of reality and may not be well adjusted enough to deal with it.

Danger Signs

No suicide should ever have to happen. Warning signs should be taken seriously. If you can recognize them, there are things you can do which will save his life.

Sometimes you may just get a feeling that something's terribly wrong: if this is the case, act on your intuition. It is better to be overly concerned than to regret that you didn't act sooner.

Matt, age 16, changed from an outgoing, sensible, friendly boy to a with-drawn and angry teenager after he split up from his first serious girl-friend. Matt's mother Lara was worried, but as his school grades remained high, teachers reassured her that this was normal 'acting out' for a boy his age. Lara wasn't convinced.

When Matt told her that he wanted to go away on holiday after his mock exams, Lara reluctantly agreed. A week before he was due to leave, Lara found entries in his diary saying that he didn't want to live anymore. She acted swiftly and ensured her son got psychiatric help. Later it emerged that Matt had planned to take his life while on holiday.

Lara followed her intuition, and in this case she was right. But what if you don't think you can rely on your intuition? What should you look out for?

- Any talk of suicide and death is a dangerous symptom. Don't ignore it. It's a myth that men who threaten suicide are attention-seeking and don't follow it through. Talking about suicide is a danger sign.
- The man you care about loses interest in everything he used to enjoy.
- He continually talks about feeling a failure, feeling worthless, or finding his life pointless.
- He starts giving away his personal possessions, or puts his affairs in order as if he is ready to die.
- He writes or changes his will.
- Any talk of death being ennobling or a relief, or references to people who have taken their own lives with a sense of identification, is a danger sign. For example, Matt in the scenario above idolized the pop star Michael Hutchence, who took his own life.
- He starts to write, paint or draw images of darkness, despair and loneliness.
- He is continually negative and incapable of seeing the positive side of things.

- He withdraws and detaches himself from all those who care about him: family, friends, partners and even pets.
- Alcohol and drug abuse has got out of hand.
- A recent loss or bereavement has shocked and traumatized him.

Jean Kerr, who founded Papyrus (Parents Association for the Prevention of Young Suicide), a voluntary organization run by parents whose sons and daughters have killed themselves, believes that there are warning signs which parents need to be alert to:

A common thread is that the individual is a very responsible, caring and sensitive person with a great sense of justice on both an individual and social level. They can have a rather uncompromising black-or-white view of things. Their behaviour is generally a little too good and rather mature for their age.
'Suicide the Lethal Epidemic that Threatens the Young', You magazine, Mail on Sunday, 19 November 2000: page 39

When warning signs are present or when your intuition tells you something is wrong, you need to act quickly. Suicidal behaviour is usually impulsive, and events can take a disastrous turn at any time. Time is not on your side.

Men and Suicide

Women attempt suicide more times than men, but men are five times more likely to actually kill themselves. According to George Murphy, a psychiatrist at the Washington School of Medicine, women's attempts at suicide stem from their desire to communicate their distress and need for help. They are more likely to make provisions for their rescue and to employ a slow means to take their lives, such as a drug overdose. They may also consider how a suicide would affect their loved ones, and so be reluctant to actually go through with it.

Unfortunately, Murphy believes that the same traits that save women's lives are interpreted as weakness and indecisiveness in men. While women seem to have the social prerogative to change their minds, men are considered deficient if they decide not to go though with the act. Reluctant to reveal how deep their despair is to others, or to acknowledge that they need help, men tend to wall themselves off from potential assistance in their time of need.

Most men don't really want to die, even though they may think that is the only answer. If you can get him treatment at the right time, you could save a depressed man's life. Always bear in mind that suicidal impulsiveness in a man is not the only solution he wants to contemplate; it is a desperate cry for help, an urgent need for treatment. You can't let him take control of the situation now. You have to take action before it is too late.

What to Do If a Man Discusses His Feelings of Suicide with You

If a man comes to you with his feelings of hopelessness, then you are clearly someone he feels he can trust. Try to remember the following points:

- He has come to you because of the person you are, so don't try to be any different. There are no right words to say; he will sense your concern. Try to remain calm and empathic. Don't argue; try to solve problems or give advice. A problem that may not seem so bad to you and easily solved may be a major life trauma to him. How he feels right now is the main point.
- Rather than trying to find the right words to say, encourage him to talk as much as possible about how he feels, and listen to him. Don't be afraid of silence. A good definition of listening is not thinking about what you are going to say. Ask open-ended

questions which require more than a 'yes' or 'no' answer. Ask about how things feel to him. Letting him unload his feelings may help him feel better.

- He may say something to you that suggests he is suicidal. Such statements can be 'I want to go to sleep now' or 'I can't go on like this anymore.' There are as many ways to say it as there are men who are depressed. If this does happen, ask in a clear, calm manner, 'Are you thinking about taking your own life?' You are not putting the idea into his head. If he hasn't considered it, he will dismiss the idea. If he has considered it, he will feel relieved that someone has realized just how hopeless and desperate he feels.

- If the answer is 'yes', ask for details. Find out how far he has got with planning this. Ask 'how' 'where' and 'when'. If he can answer these specifics, he is probably seriously considering suicide as an option. Remember, though, that if you are in any doubt, seek advice rather than trying to diagnose the condition yourself.

Most of the time the advice given so far has been to accept when a man is showing strong emotion, but there are times when you need to take emergency action. Perhaps he is putting himself or other people in danger. Perhaps you feel out of your depth or that he has totally lost control. In an emergency, call for help.

Continue to offer a listening ear, but also be clear that he needs to get professional help. Reassure him if he is nervous about this that you are not going to leave him alone and that you will go with him. You could try your doctor, your local health centre, the casualty department of a hospital, or a crisis helpline like the Samaritans. Tell him suicide is not the solution, and that getting help is. Tell him you are taking how he feels very seriously. Go with him to seek help, and stay with him until medical experts arrive.

If he resists and won't seek help, you can step aside or you can intervene to stop him. Again, this has to be your choice, but if you do want to intervene, call the emergency services immediately.

A Legacy of Pain

Men who commit suicide have taken steps to ensure that they are not discovered until after the act has been completed. Having said that, most men while contemplating suicide do try to raise the subject with a relative, friend or doctor.

If you are worried that a man you care about may be thinking about taking his own life, give him lots of opportunities to talk to you. Don't overdo it, but be persistent.

If he seems isolated, encourage him to join in things, and keep asking him and inviting him even if he refuses. Try to understand and accept what he says, and help him explore possible ways to sort himself out. Be as supportive as you can. Learn about the condition and don't expect him to snap back to his old self overnight. Encourage him to seek professional help, or at least to unburden himself to an anonymous telephone line, and keep reminding him that depression can be treated.

To take his own life a man must be in extreme turmoil, and that turmoil becomes his legacy to those he leaves behind. 'I feel like half a person,' says Adam, whose father hung himself. 'Every day the pain is with me. I get up with it. I exist with it. I go to bed with it,' says Marcia, whose partner Bill jumped in front of a train. 'I can't see a future. It doesn't exist for me,' says Andrea, whose son Toby died from an overdose on his seventeenth birthday.

Knowing that you did the best you could will offer some comfort, but coping with the legacy of the suicide of a man you cared about is one of the most harrowing and traumatic of experiences. Hopefully, with the help of this book and the support of your doctor, it is an experience you will never have to go through.

10

What Treatments Are Available?

Most therapists, counsellors and doctors today treat depressed patients by taking into account all areas of their lives. If a man you know is depressed, you will continue to play an important part in his recovery, and it is important that you understand what treatment is available and what to expect.

Therapy

Therapy has lost much of its stigma. The enormous demand for therapy, which seems to be growing every year, has made it acceptable. Psychotherapy broadly means 'talking cure' – a client talking through their problems with a therapist – but it's actually a term used for a wide range and scale of therapies and practitioners. Certification and licensing vary from region to region, so you need to exercise care in finding a therapist with adequate training.

Many lives are enriched and repaired by therapy, but an unskilled therapist can be far more damaging than no therapist at all. A man who sees a therapist is in a vulnerable position, so it's important to ensure that his vulnerability is not exposed or exploited. If he is considering therapy and wants to get something organized without first seeing a doctor, it's important that he and you are informed and educated about the different kinds of therapy available.

Psychiatry

This therapy is concerned with the diagnosis and treatment of mental disorders. A psychiatrist is a medical doctor who has done further training in psychiatry. Treatment will involve a combination of drugs and therapy. It is important that you are aware that a psychiatrist is the *only* therapist who can prescribe drugs on prescription.

Psychiatry is suitable for men with a recognized clinical depression or other mental illness such as schizophrenia.

A psychiatrist must have completed a medical degree with a training programme in psychiatry, as opposed to another speciality such as paediatrics. Not all psychiatrists have much experience in psychotherapy, but some do. In past decades, psychiatric training emphasized the *physical* causes of depression, and treatment was with medication only. As a result, the psychiatric community is increasingly divided between those who favour the biological explanation for emotional or mental illness, and those who favour more psychological causes, and who therefore practise psychotherapy (see below). Some psychiatrists work closely with a psychologist or therapist who provides the psychotherapy portion of the treatment.

Psychology

This branch of medicine is concerned with human behaviour. It is illegal for someone without training or qualifications to be called a chartered or licensed psychologist. Psychology is suitable for people with psychological distress or mental problems, including anxiety, phobias, obsessive compulsive behaviours, or addictive behaviour.

Many clinical psychologists work in private practice, but they are also found in health centres, hospitals and community centres. Counselling psychologists work with relationship problems and family issues. Educational psychologists deal with children with emotional or social problems and learning difficulties. Occupational psychologists help companies with training, motivation and matters such as stress and workplace bullying.

With a psychologist, look for the qualifications 'chartered' or 'licensed'. The British Psychological Society publishes a register of chartered psychologists; this is available at libraries or on their website (see Resources chapter). In the US you need to contact the American Psychological Association to find out more about requirements for licensing, or you can call your state education department, division of professional licensing services, for the requirements demanded by your state.

Psychotherapy

Traditional psychotherapy, called psychoanalytic psychotherapy, is the original talking cure. In the classic scenario, a man sits facing his therapist, discussing his problems. Each session lasts for an hour, and the treatment can last for months or years. It is based on the principles of psychoanalysis, placing importance on a patient's early life experiences and exploring their thoughts, feelings, dreams and memories. The psychotherapist's skill is to listen carefully and to suggest new ways of seeing patterns or thought-behaviour.

Psychotherapy is suitable for men with depression, anxiety, relationship problems, eating disorders, obsessive behaviour and low self-esteem. The aim of a good psychotherapist is to be a guide and support for a man to find his own solutions. Woody Allen has famously spent a lifetime and a fortune on this one, but for most people psychotherapy lasts a few years. It can be more probing than counselling (see below), and sessions (usually once a week or more) are designed to focus on the source of his depression or unhappiness.

When seeking a psychotherapist in the UK, look for accreditation from either the UK Council for Psychotherapy or the British Association for Counselling and Psychotherapy. Training takes a minimum of three years. Either can inform you about qualified psychotherapists (see Resources chapter).

In the US there are no rules or restrictions about who can call themselves a psychotherapist. If you are referred to someone who calls themselves a psychotherapist, be sure to ask questions about their training to determine if they are suitable. In some states, social workers are trained in psychotherapy. Check with your state authorities that the social worker is licensed and certified to be a psychotherapist.

It's impossible to describe all the various forms of psychotherapy in this book (for further information, see Resources chapter), but one form is often cited as an effective tool for beating depression, and that is cognitive behavioural therapy, developed by a University of Pennsylvania psychiatrist, Aaron T Beck.

Cognitive Behavioural Therapy

Cognitive therapy focuses on practical techniques – changing thought processes and behaviour to solve specific problems. It does not try to alter your moods; rather, it tries to find ways of altering how you look at the things that are causing your moods. For example, a man may be depressed over the fear of heart trouble, and interpret perfectly natural aches and pains as meaning disease. A cognitist, having identified such beliefs, would show the man how his thinking was wrong – showing him, for example, how his aches and pains could be due to poor posture or muscular strain.

Cognitive behavioural therapists believe that thoughts affect feelings and vice versa. The therapist would use this approach to help the man you care about focus on self-defeating automatic thoughts such as 'I'm a failure' and the unconscious belief system behind them.

Cognitive behavioural therapy can appeal to men suffering from depression. Negative thoughts are analysed, as you would analyse the hypothesis of a scientific experiment. They are taken apart and tested bit by bit. Beliefs are explored together, tested, and finally changed.

For instance, if a man thinks he is a failure, a therapist might ask 'Are you a failure in every aspect of your life?' or 'Think of something you succeeded doing last month.' The therapist helps a man recognize for himself that his thoughts may be illogical, distorted, one-sided or faulty. When he is able to recognize this, he can then start challenging his negative thinking so that his feelings about himself improve.

The work a man does outside of his therapy sessions will be as important as the time spent in them. He will be given 'assignments' each week, many of which you may be asked to be involved in. These assignments can consist of listing negative thoughts that occur during the day, reading material about depression, reviewing the therapy sessions on tape, writing, role-playing and so on. The man you care about may be required to ask you to help him point out his automatic self-critical statements. This can be an enlightening exercise for you too, as you start to become aware of your own negative thought patterns.

If the man you care about decides on cognitive behavioural therapy, you can support and encourage him without nagging or becoming too involved. Bear in mind that as he learns new ways of thinking and behaving, his progress may be erratic. Your role is to applaud his progress, however small it might seem.

Cognitive behavioural therapy is suitable for depression, but it is most successful for phobias and stress-management.

Brief Therapy

Brief therapy refers to a combination of therapeutic techniques used over a short period of time. It often involves cognitive behavioural techniques along with elements of analytical thinking or counselling. It is suitable for specific stress-related problems. The therapy is very goal-oriented and practical. That doesn't mean, however, that there isn't opportunity to explore feelings or past experiences.

Counselling

Counsellors often work in clinics or institutional settings along with other mental health professionals. There can be some confusion about the distinction between therapists and counsellors. Sometimes the difference involves qualifications or training, but more often it refers to a different theoretical approach.

As a general rule, counselling is shorter term, and may be focused around particular issues which have arisen out of the past or present. It can enable a person to find solutions or insights into particular areas of his or her life. Counsellors can be seen as professionals who can help with emotional problems such as low self-esteem, loss, bereavement or addiction. During the course of the sessions, a counsellor will help a person look at patterns of behaviour which are stopping him or her getting the most out of life. Sessions are usually just under an hour long, and last for a period of time agreed between the client and counsellor.

FINDING THE RIGHT COUNSELLOR

A doctor can give the man you care about a direct referral to a counsellor if this is advised. There may be one attached to the doctor's practice, or you may be given a list of available counsellors in your area. Usually counsellors who are attached to doctors' practices will see clients in a room attached to the surgery. You will probably be offered about six sessions. Counsellors who are employed as part of a doctor's practice or health centre will have had their qualifications and references checked.

Finding the right counsellor may be a process of trial and error. Counsellors follow a range of theoretical backgrounds or 'models'. The man you care about may find this confusing at times, but he shouldn't be put off by wondering where they are coming from. At the heart of the counselling process is helping the individual who is having the sessions. A counsellor is there to help the client look at how problems are presenting themselves, and how to start to find a way through them.

Should the man you care about wish to go into longer-term counselling after the first set of sessions, he could ask about continuing. If he needs to look elsewhere, the British Association for Counselling and Psychotherapy (see Resources chapter) has lists of counsellors throughout the country. There is also a reference directory on the internet of qualified and registered practitioners (see 'Psychotherapy Register' in the Resources chapter).

Above all, before the man you care about starts any counselling or therapy, it is important to check that the counsellor or therapist he is going to see is properly trained and qualified. The British Association for Counselling and Psychotherapy, and also the UK Council for Psychotherapy, can give him and you further information.

In the US, the term 'counsellor' is used to describe wide variety of different mental health professionals. They often work in the clinics of institutional settings along with other mental health professionals. Some counsellors hold a C.A.C., which means they are certified to counsel people on alcohol and drugs, but in most states there are no uniform licences or certification required to call oneself a counsellor. Check that the counsellor has experience working with people who are mentally ill, and a Bachelor's or Associate's degree in psychology, counselling or a related field.

What to Look for in a Good Therapist

As a significant other, you can't become involved in the counselling or therapeutic process itself, but the man you care about may wish to consider the following points which may arise out of the initial assessment session. Remember that confidentiality is a pre-condition of the therapeutic relationship between him and the counsellor, so your involvement may only be in a supportive role.

The following are some easy, but pertinent, questions that he should consider at the first session, and when thinking about it afterwards, which will help to evaluate if the sessions are going to help and if they are ethical.

- What code of ethics does the therapist/counsellor follow, and which professional body is he or she accountable to? The British Association for Counselling and Psychotherapy and the UK Council for Psychotherapy have specific codes of practice which ensure professional standards.
- Does the counsellor or therapist have professional, clinical supervision which is also an essential part of the therapeutic process?
- Does the counsellor or therapist have a procedure for referral should he or she need extra support?
- Does the man you care about have an idea of what he wishes to get from counselling or therapy?
- If more sessions have been decided upon, is there a clearly stated number of sessions or 'contract' agreed between the counsellor/therapist and client?

After the first session, the man you care about should have a clearer idea of what to expect. You may be able to help here if he wishes to discuss his general feelings about the counselling process. The following questions may be helpful to him to evaluate whether to continue or not:

- Did it feel right generally? Was the counselling room quiet, calm and conducive to talking?
- Did he feel that he was listened to and supported in the session?
- Did he get confirmation of which code of confidentiality and ethics the counsellor works to?
- How did it feel to sit and talk about himself for a length of time without any personal information being given by the counsellor about him- or herself? Remember that counselling and therapy is not having a conversation. It is a means of enabling clients to explore their feelings and life in a safe, non-judgemental setting.

Underlying the counselling and therapeutic process should be the belief that the man you care about can work towards managing his depression in a way that will help him to take back control of his life. You can support him in this by being reassuring and, when he starts to feel stronger, by stepping back and giving him the space he needs to take more control over his treatment.

Intervention is necessary if the man you care about makes moves to harm himself. It is probable that your doctor will be alerted to any suicide attempt. If the man you care for is in counselling and therapy during the period of time that he makes such an attempt, he may choose to disclose this to his counsellor – it is not for you to do so on his behalf, as it remains his concern. Clients are usually asked at assessment for a contact number in case of emergency; the man you care about may choose you or someone else. Counsellors may, in turn, wish to alert other services if they feel there is a high level of risk, but this should be done with the informed consent of the client. At all times, remember that the counselling process is confidential between the client (i.e. the man you care about) and the counsellor.

Bear in mind that the process of change can take time. Some clients find that counselling or therapy helps them greatly, others find it is not for them at this point in their lives. Again, it remains the decision of the man you care about.

How Much Will it Cost?

Prices vary enormously depending on the kind of therapy, where the man you care about lives, and how long it will take. Psychiatrists tend to be the most expensive. In the US, a psychiatrist's fee ranges from $150 to $200 or more an hour. Generally, a psychotherapist charges about half that, with a psychologist's fee somewhere in the middle. In the UK, psychotherapy costs from £25 to £50 an hour; cognitive behavioural therapy from £30 to £120. Fees tend to be higher in private practice than in either a clinic or hospital-based outpatient settings. Some counsellors and psychotherapists offer a 'sliding scale' of fees dependent on the client's income and circumstances.

Not being able to afford therapy does not have to stop you from getting help for the man you care about, but it certainly can present problems. Always check what kind of treatment his insurance covers. As his supporter, you can ask about fee reduction. It's a laborious process, but it is possible to get some kind of financial relief.

Counselling and therapy in the UK is available on the NHS and, increasingly, through doctors' referral. Waiting lists can be long, but it is an increasingly growing part of doctors' practices.

Organizations such as Relate ask for a donation based on what you can afford. The Samaritans run a free 24-hour helpline to discuss such issues (see Resources chapter).

Many corporations and insurance companies will pay for cognitive behavioural therapy treatment, and some therapists offer a sliding scale of charges depending on your circumstances. In the US, some clinics also offer sliding scale fees. If you live near a major research centre, the man you care about may be able to participate in an ongoing research project.

Will It Be Good for Him to Talk?

For centuries there was no other option for depression but to talk about it. Sigmund Freud and others proposed theories of human behaviour based on childhood experiences, and we now take for granted that early upbringing, frustrated desires and sexual conflicts may underlie adult emotional states, and that events from our past can influence how we feel.

One perception of psychotherapy is that it takes too long for observable change. It can take time for improvement to show itself. Few men have the time or the money for extended therapy, which can continue for years. Group therapy and brief psychotherapy are now more popular, but even these still last for months and are aimed at discovering how past experiences can influence your mood.

Psychotherapy is one of the most effective treatments for depression, but some experts believe that counselling and therapy are more of a hinder than a help for men who are depressed. They believe that it can stop a man taking control of his life, and encourage dependency and self-blame. Much depends on the man and his individual circumstances, but studies show that it is dangerous to bottle up emotions. If a depressed man can acknowledge his feelings in therapy, he is making the first step on the road to recovery.

To benefit from talking therapies, it helps if the man is willing to talk about his problems and has some insight into his psychological makeup. If the man you care about does decide to see a therapist, it may involve having to explore painful emotions. He also needs to be patient. Acknowledging emotions in a structured way can help change negative emotions, but it's not a miracle cure and won't happen overnight.

It can be frustrating to have some counselling and psychotherapy and not see immediate results. If the man you care about is concerned about this, he should ask his counsellor or therapist to review at different stages, so that he can see his own progress. Or he should talk to his doctor about additional help available. This help may involve some form of medication.

Medication for Depression

The most effective treatment for severe depression is a combination of therapy and antidepressant medication. According to the American Psychiatric Association, patients with mild or moderate depression usually benefit from therapy alone. However, if symptoms persist for more than 20 sessions, or get worse, medication is necessary.

Imbalances in certain brain chemicals called neurotransmitters – especially serotonin, dopamine and norepinephrine – are thought to be linked with depression. Antidepressant medication attempts to regulate these imbalances.

Antidepressants have a bad reputation, perhaps because the drugs used in the 1950s and 1960s had many side-effects and masked symptoms rather than treating them. The man you care about may worry that he will become addicted, or that taking medication is a sign of weakness. But the antidepressants used today are not tranquilizers nor 'uppers'; nor are they addictive. They can be highly effective, with a success rate of up to 80 per cent. They are able to relieve feelings of hopelessness and despair, and alleviate other symptoms like insomnia, anxiety and fatigue. They can also ease the uncontrollable highs of mania. Taking them is no more a sign of weakness than taking insulin for diabetes.

Antidepressant medication can only be prescribed by a physician, which means a doctor or a psychiatrist, a psychopharmacologist or biopsychiatrist. It can be prescribed in combination with therapy, and in this case the physician may work in close contact with the therapist to monitor a patient's progress.

In most, but not all cases, a doctor will usually initiate certain tests, including a neurological exam and some lab tests, to determine if there are any physiological causes for depression, if there is evidence of substance abuse, to check the functions of vital organs and to determine the best course of treatment. Expect the man you care about to be monitored monthly or weekly. At each visit, his blood levels will be tested and his progress monitored.

It's hard to predict what kind of medication will be most effective. Some men respond well to one drug and not to another. Each man's response to treatment will be unique. His doctor may well have to try a variety of different medications until the right one is found. Both you and the man you care about will need to be patient and flexible in your approach.

Once a course of medication is begun, insomnia tends to lessen in the first week or so. The other symptoms take a few weeks more to abate. Because the medication improves mood, the man you care about may be tempted to abandon treatment. If this is the case, you need to urge him to take his medication as directed. Effectiveness depends on the drug being taken regularly. Doctors often keep depressed patients on medication for 4 to 12 months after symptoms have diminished, to ensure there is no relapse.

There can be side-effects at times, which the man you care about should be informed of. These include weight gain, rashes, dry mouth, stomach upset, loss of libido and palpitations. Unfortunately, these symptoms sometimes appear before symptoms start to abate, and this could make him unwilling to continue. Hopefully he will have been warned that this may be the case and will persevere. However, he should ask his doctor before starting any treatment, so that he knows what to expect.

Medication takes a few weeks to become fully effective and to reach the right level in the bloodstream – called the therapeutic dosage. This can vary from man to man and, as mentioned earlier, the search for the correct treatment dosage takes time. Older men will metabolize their medication much more slowly than younger men, so the therapeutic dose accumulates faster.

It can take up to six months or more to find the correct medication and dosage, so the man you care about needs to be patient. Your support and encouragement during this period of trial and error could prove crucial.

Now let's briefly look at some of the most commonly prescribed depression medications.

CYCLIC ANTIDEPRESSANTS

Cyclic antidepressants block the absorption or reuptake of the neurotransmitters norepinephrine and serotonin. The drugs Tofranil (generic name: imipramine), Elavil (amitriptyline) and Ludiomil (maprotiline) are cyclic antidepressants.

Common side-effects of cyclic antidepressants include dry mouth, constipation, blurry vision, drowsiness, insomnia, weight gain and dizziness. They may also reduce libido and cause sweating or nausea, and difficulty urinating. The man you care about should ask his doctor about how he can lessen these side-effects. If medication is taken at bedtime, some of the side-effects may occur while he is asleep.

SSRIs

SSRIs, selective serotonin reuptake inhibitors, are newer medications that belong to the cyclic antidepressants group. Lack of serotonin is believed to underlie depression. Low levels are associated with suicidal behaviour, impulsiveness, aggression and violence, and high levels are associated with leadership qualities. SSRIs allow for higher levels of serotonin to circulate in the body.

SSRIs have become widely used in recent years. Brand names include Prozac (fluoxetine) and Zoloft (sertraline). They are popular because they seem to act more quickly and have fewer side-effects than earlier cyclic medications. They are less interactive with other medications, are much less likely to cause drowsiness and poor concentration, and they lift mood reliably and safely.

MAOIs

Monoamine Oxidase Inhibitor Antidepressants (MAOIs) include the medications Marplan (isocarboxazid), Nardil (phenelzine) and Parnate (tranylcypromine). These try to correct an imbalance of neurotransmitters called monoamines in the brain. Monoamines affect the absorption of serotonin and norepinephrine. Low levels of monoamines are associated with depression.

MAOIs can be effective, but they carry more risks than SSRIs. Side-effects include high blood pressure and strokes, which can cause death. If the man you care about is suicidal, an overdose of MAOIs can be lethal, so medication needs to be controlled.

Monoamines also occur in other parts of the body, and in certain foods, so to avoid dangerously high levels men who take MAOIs must avoid yoghurt, pickled, smoked or fermented meats and fish (such as herring), cheeses such as cheddar, Swiss and parmesan (cottage cheese and cream cheese are safe), liver, beer, wine or sherry, caffeine, tinned figs, Marmite, bovril or other yeast or meat extracts. The doctor will provide dietary guidelines along with the prescription.

Taking other medications alongside MAOIs is also a potential risk, so the man you care about must tell his psychiatrist about any drugs, even over-the-counter ones, he is taking at the same time.

LITHIUM

Lithium is most often prescribed for patients suffering from manic-depression (also known as bipolar disorder). It is thought that lithium can affect neurotransmitters in the brain, and the drug is effective in about 70 per cent of cases. It takes about a week to be effective. Side-effects include urinary problems, poor co-ordination, nausea, tremors and tiredness.

ECT

Electroconvulsive Therapy (ECT) conjures up images of shock treatment by men in white coats to patients in padded cells, but today ECT is given while the patient is sedated and given a short-term anaesthetic so no pain is felt. ECT is used only for severely depressed patients who have engaged in a suicide attempt or are exhibiting psychotic behaviour. Treatment takes place over a period of days, and mild electrical currents are used to affect the parts of the brain that are linked to depression in an attempt to 'jolt' a man out of his depression. There is a risk of memory loss and confusion after treatment, although this is usually short term.

When Medication Is Refused

In some cases you may find that because the medication evens out his moods, a man may actually miss the intensity of his previous highs and lows. This is especially the case with manic-depressives, who have become addicted to their intoxicating highs. In other cases the man you care about may simply forget that he needs to take his drugs, or may feel so hopeless that he stops taking medication in the belief that therapy and medication can't help him.

Sometimes a man stops taking his medication because he feels better or because the side-effects make him feel worse, but as explained earlier this is not advisable. To be effective, medication needs to be taken regularly, and it's often the case that a man will feel worse before he feels better.

You can't force a man to take medication if he doesn't want to, but you can encourage him to continue with his treatment. You can also inform the doctor if you notice that he isn't taking his medication, so that appropriate steps can be taken.

Why Should He Take Antidepressants?

There is concern that too many doctors are dishing out antidepressants rather than spending time talking to their patients. Prescriptions for drugs like Prozac and Zoloft, which have minimal side-effects and can offer relief within days, are at an all-time high. Millions of people now take antidepressants.

While it is regrettable but true that overworked doctors simply haven't got time to talk at length to patients, a good doctor will never prescribe antidepressants for the sake of it. He or she should only offer drugs when a man simply can't seem to lift his curtain of gloom. Antidepressants can kick-start treatment so that a man can see that he doesn't have to feel the way he does and that treatment can help. Once his mood is lifted enough, he may be better able to respond to the help of others.

Like therapy, antidepressants are not a magic solution, but they are part of the answer.

Your Support Is Crucial

You may be the person who got the man to visit a doctor in the first place. Someone who is depressed may find that their motivation dissipates, and in this sense you must give him guidance. You can be an important link between patient and doctor by ensuring that appointments are kept, tablets taken as prescribed, that the man avoids making major decisions, and by reinforcing the doctor's or therapist's assurances of a good outcome.

If well-meaning friends and family tell the man you are looking after to 'snap out of it' or 'pull himself together,' discourage this kind of pressure; it is harmful. A sympathetic and understanding attitude is needed throughout. While waiting for his treatment to take effect, your contact can be a lifeline to a depressed man, lost as he is in an emotional vacuum. You should encourage him to keep active, if necessary by sharing some of his chores.

Should you find that your best efforts are futile and are not making any impact, then the depression has reached a dangerous phase. If the man you care about is thinking about taking his own life, let the doctor know. He or she will advise you on the necessary precautions. Talk of suicide must always be taken seriously. Constant reassurance is a great comfort and can help counter his negativity, but if you feel that you can't watch over him as he becomes severely depressed and thus limit the risk of suicide, then he is best off being cared for in a hospital.

Hospitalization

Hospitalization will occur only if the man you care about becomes a danger to himself or those around him. A man can't be forced to have treatment unless he is judged to be so depressed that the risk of suicide is high. In these circumstances, he may be legally committed to a psychiatric hospital.

Hospitalization isn't imprisonment; it offers a safe, structured environment where a man can be treated on a daily basis. You may worry constantly if being in hospital is the right step for him, and visits may be upsetting, but on the plus side you know he is safe and is being helped by experts. The hospital may also offer support groups and counselling, which can make him feel less isolated.

Addictive Behaviours

Alcohol and drug addiction are serious and often tragic problems that can ruin lives, careers and relationships. If you know that the man you care about has a drug or alcohol problem, seek professional help.

It is usually obvious when a man is addicted to alcohol and drugs, but if it is not, be aware if he shows noticeable mood swings, is sometimes aggressive, is constantly short of money (he may be stealing to support his habit) and is evasive when questioned. Get advice from your doctor, who may be able to direct you to various support groups in your area.

Alcoholics Anonymous can provide structured support programmes for many men in combination with psychotherapy. The steps towards his recovery are action-oriented and specific. The programme also combats isolation, and he may develop a rapport with other members of the group, or with a 'sponsor' who can give him non-judgemental, experienced support. Allied groups for family members, such as Al-Anon, can also be helpful. These groups help to clarify enabling or co-dependent aspects of relationships, and also give you support in times of crisis and need.

A compulsion to gamble is also relatively common and can have severely destructive effects on a man's career, family life and personal relationships. If he regularly gambles and risks far more than he can afford, if he steals to support a gambling habit, or feels compelled to gamble, then once again, seek professional advice. Talk to your doctor or contact Gamblers Anonymous – the address will be in your phone book.

Almost anything can become the focus of compulsive behaviour: caffeine, sex, exercise, food. If the man you care about is dependent on a substance, legal or illegal, he may not recognize that he is addicted. Pointing this out to him and encouraging him to quit may be all that is required. If not, and you are concerned about his health, talk to your doctor.

In recent years, with all the discussion of dependencies and co-dependencies within relationships, it is often assumed that women tend to be co-dependants. However, men can also get jealous, compulsive and manipulative.

Interdependence is a good thing; couples need each other. When the dependence becomes one-sided, however, other warning signs may appear. If the man you care about becomes totally dependent and abuses that fact, or tries to control you with emotional blackmail, this is an unequal relationship. If you find that your life is totally wrapped up with the man you care about and it is making you depressed, you may be depending on him too much for feelings of self-worth.

A relationship turns co-dependent when the anxiety of the carer gets jumbled up with the person who is depressed, creating misery and confusion for both parties. Neither of you will feel able to end or leave the relationship – both are trapped in dependency.

Problems in relationships often arise because members of a couple need to communicate their needs, wants, hopes and anxieties to each other. If this is a problem for you, try to improve the communication between you (see Chapter 6). If you have tried to resolve problems and your emotional life is still dominated by compulsive or obsessive feelings, neither of you is in control and you need professional help. Talk to your doctor or seek advice from a relationship counsellor or therapist (see Resources chapter).

Treatment for Elation

If the man you care about suffers from episodes of elation as well as depression, his condition takes on an added urgency. He may be unaware of his altered mood state when he is in a manic phase of depression, and is likely to vehemently resist seeing a doctor. The responsibility then falls on you or others who care about him to contend with a man whose judgement is gradually deteriorating and who is acting out of character.

If the elation is mild, the man may simply need advice about how to avoid potential hazards. He may be unaware of the change, so it might be best to mention it to him, but be careful how you word it. If the mood change is more pronounced and there is a realistic understanding of the need for treatment, medication can be prescribed without recourse to hospitalization. The doctor may be interested to hear your objective account, to assess the extent of mood changes in his patient. If you or someone else he is close to can monitor his mood changes, keep a record of his medication and communicate with the doctor, there is generally a successful outcome.

If he becomes dangerously hyperactive in his elation phase – for instance driving recklessly and putting his own life and those of others at risk – or severely depressed in his depressed phase, this may mean admittance to hospital.

If medication is advised, anti-elation tablets will be prescribed. Phenothiazines have a profoundly sedative effect and have much in common with cyclic antidepressants in that they try to correct chemical imbalances in the brain and have few side-effects. Calming drugs include Largactil (chlorpromazine), Sparine (promazine) and Melleril (thioridazine). Serenace or Haldol (haloperidol) is a more potent anti-elatant drug and has a particularly rapid effect on racing thoughts and hyperactivity.

The main side-effects of these drugs involve the body muscles. Normal, spontaneous movements of the face, arms and other muscles is diminished, producing a still appearance and drooling of saliva. Other side-effects include drowsiness, blurred vision and rashes. But such side-effects can be kept to a minimum by reducing the dosage or taking antidotes. Lithium is also used to dramatically limit the length of elation, and it is relatively free of side-effects. However, because it takes up to two weeks to take effect, other anti-elatant tablets may need to be taken in the meantime.

What Does Alternative Therapy Have to Offer?

Certain alternative remedies claim to be able to relieve the symptoms of depression and create a feeling of physical and emotional well-being. If the man you care about is interested, some of the major therapies for depression are listed below. Many alternative therapists will offer advice on diet and lifestyle, in line with the recommendations given in Chapter 7.

The therapies listed here all adhere to the principle of holism – the body, mind, spirit and emotions as interdependent parts of the whole person. If a man is depressed, most alternative therapists will want to build up a picture of his whole life and his unique constitution to make a diagnosis.

ALEXANDER TECHNIQUE

This is a system of re-education that is aimed at helping the man you care about regain his natural balance, posture and ease of movement and to eliminate habits of slouching or slumping. He will be taught new ways of using his body, and encouraged to think about new ways of keeping his spine free of tension.

The Alexander Technique can help with depression and stress-related conditions, including fatigue and anxiety. The depressed stance of slumped shoulders and a lowered head can contribute significantly to feelings of low self-esteem. It's harder to feel depressed when you stand tall with your head high.

AROMATHERAPY

Aromatherapy involves the use of oils extracted from plants, herbs and trees such as lavender, rosemary and sandalwood to promote physical and emotional well-being. It is often used in conjunction with massage. Oils can be rubbed into his skin or added to his bath. Oils most often recommended for depression are sandalwood, chamomile, lavender, rose, clary sage and bergamot.

AUTOGENIC TRAINING

The man you care about might consider autogenic training – a gentle form of self-administered psychotherapy which teaches special mental exercises to help him relax mentally and physically and replace negative thoughts with positive ones.

AYURVEDA

Ayurveda is a Sanskrit word for 'science of life'. This ancient Indian therapy is a comprehensive health-care system and incorporates detoxification, diet, exercise, breathing, meditation, massage and herbs. Herbs are used as part of remedies designed to correct different sorts of energy imbalances in the body. Depression is believed to be a symptom of such imbalances, and an important aim of the skilled practitioner is to eliminate them. Yoga can be a significant part of Ayurveda (see below).

BACH FLOWER REMEDIES

There are 38 different flower remedies, all widely available in chemists and health stores. The remedies are good for health and balancing emotional, spiritual and psychological states such as uncertainty, indecision and despondency. Bach Rescue Remedy combines the benefits of several flowers and acts as a sort of quick boost for men under stress. For sudden depression with no obvious cause, Mustard is often recommended.

BREATHING

Breathing gives us the oxygen we need to produce energy and renew cells, and expels three quarter of the body's waste. Many Eastern therapists believe that when we breathe in we draw in positive energy, and when we breathe out we expel negative energy.

Depression and stress can cause breathing to deteriorate, so that it fails to cleanse the mind and body. Depression tends to make the breathing very shallow, when a person should breathe deeply. Encourage the man you care about to pay attention to his breathing: He should breathe fully and from the chest and belly. If he breathes in a calm way, his body may think he is calm, and stress levels may reduce.

TRADITIONAL CHINESE MEDICINE

Herbalism, together with t'ai chi and acupuncture, form the basis of traditional Chinese medicine, a system of health care still widely practised in Hong Kong, China and in some states in the US. Herbs are used to prevent ill-health and to treat both mental and physical illness and to balance emotional upset. Ginseng is a well-known Chinese remedy to stimulate energy. Tiger balm is used to relieve aches and pains.

A doctor of Chinese medicine will recommend the herbs that address a patient's particular imbalances which are contributing to depression. Because the effects are gentle, improvement is seen only after several weeks or several months of treatment.

Acupuncture

Acupuncture involves using needles to stimulate points in the body called acupoints. It is thought that these points rest at significant junctions of energy limes which form a sort of network of the flow of vital energy through the body. It is believed that depression causes or is caused by blockages in these vital energy points. The practitioner selects points based on the diagnosis and goals of treatment.

HERBALISM

Medicinal herbalism uses the curative properties of various parts of plants, such as flowers, bark, nuts, seeds and herbs, to maintain good health and treat disease. Herbs can be taken in a variety of forms – tinctures, teas, infusions, creams, ointments, capsules, etc. St John's Wort, also sold over the counter as Kira, is used to treat depression (see below).

RELAXATION TECHNIQUES

Helping the man you care about incorporate a relaxation technique into his daily life will have a positive benefit on his health, lower his blood pressure and help regulate mood swings. Of the therapies listed here, aromatherapy, massage, meditation, yoga and t'ai chi are helpful in promoting relaxation.

ST JOHN'S WORT

St John's Wort (*Hypericum perforatum*) is a herb that is widely used and prescribed in Europe for depression. It is emerging as one of the most popular, effective and safest antidepressants – perhaps even more popular than conventional antidepressants.

For example, in Germany it is the number one antidepressant prescribed by doctors, far outselling Prozac. Every year German doctors write 3 million prescriptions for St John's Wort, as compared with 240,000 for Prozac. It could become an astonishing alternative to the drugs now used in the US and UK to treat depression.

St John's Wort is a naturally occurring herb, not the result of pharmaceutical development. It does appear to help many people suffering from depression, with minimal side-effects. Research on St John's Wort is still in its infancy, but recent studies show that it may affect the transmission of the neurotransmitters serotonin, norepinephrine and dopamine, which are thought to play a role in depression. Most conventional antidepressants don't have such a unified effect.

St John's Wort is available over the counter, unlike other antidepressants which need a prescription from a doctor. For the depressed man who would previously not want to seek medical help, perhaps out of feelings of shame, fear or stigma, St John's Wort may well be a boon. On the other hand, if a man is seriously depressed he really needs the wisdom, support and guidance of a skilled psychiatrist. If he self-medicates unsuccessfully he may delay his recovery or suffer all manner of setbacks in the process.

St John's Wort may well play a role in recovery if the man you care about suffers from mild to moderate depression. If his symptoms are severe, it is best to seek the advice of a doctor or psychiatrist.

The target dose in most antidepressant studies of mild to moderate depression is 900 mg of Hypericum a day, and the Kira® brand is most often recommended. Side-effects are rare, but may include stomach upsets, fatigue and, less commonly, allergic reactions. It can also interact with other drugs, so if the man you care about is on medication, ask the pharmacist or your doctor for advice. St John's Wort should *not* be used alongside other antidepressants.

It's perhaps best to start with a lower dose and build up, but self-medication is a tricky business. Each man will react differently.

St John's Wort is being hailed as a wonder drug by some enthusiasts, but it is important not to put all your hopes on one treatment alone and to keep an open mind. Some people don't feel better after taking it. If it does not appear to be working after two weeks, the man you care about should see a doctor.

Being properly informed is crucial if the man you care about wants to try St John's Wort. You will find information about the herb in books about the medicinal properties of herbs, and Dr Norman Rosenthal's *St John's Wort: Your Natural Prozac* is an invaluable guide that will tell you everything you need to know about the herb, how to it can help, how to take it, what the side-effects are, and how to monitor progress on it.

HOMOEOPATHY

The art of treating 'like with like', homoeopathy relies on the belief that a substance which causes particular symptoms can also be used, in minute doses, to cure those same symptoms. Remedies are derived by diluting in (water and alcohol) sources taken from plants, minerals and animals. Homoeopaths prefer to treat each case individually, but Natrum mur is often recommended when a person thinks constantly of past sad events. Ignatia, Pulsatilla and Sulphur may also help lift mood.

HYPNOTHERAPY

Hypnotherapy can be a powerful aid for those fighting addictions to alcohol, cigarettes or drugs, for those suffering traumas or phobias, and for those wanting to boost self-image. A hypnotherapist can induce a light trance in the client, which can bring to consciousness repressed emotions – particularly helpful in the case of depression. In this light trance state a man can become receptive to suggestions which can help him accept or reject patterns of belief or behaviour – also helpful for depression. In unskilled hands hypnotherapy may be unwise, so make sure a therapist is chosen carefully.

MASSAGE

Most men are delighted to receive massages, and a massage has well-known stress-relieving and relaxational effects. One form of massage, built on the philosophy of acupuncture, is acupressure. In acupressure the acupoints are stimulated to alleviate depression. Pressure points associated with depression include a point which lies four-fingers' width from the inside of the ankle, and a point two-fingers' width from either side of the spine, just below the shoulder blades.

MEDITATION

Meditation and visualization are contemplative techniques which can calm and clear an overactive mind. During meditation, brainwaves change to a distinctive pattern linked with deep relaxation and mental alertness. Regular meditators can shift into this mode at will, allowing them to deal efficiently with stress.

It is one of life's ironies that those who would benefit most from meditation are invariably the ones most resistant to it. If a man is depressed, meditation isn't likely to appeal to him, but studies show that meditation can reduce stress, anxiety and depression.

NUTRITIONAL THERAPY

Nutritional therapy uses diet and vitamin and mineral supplementation to balance the body and prevent illness. There are three basic diagnoses: food intolerances, nutritional deficiencies, and toxic overload. The most common food intolerances are to wheat, dairy produce, nuts, eggs, yeast, shellfish, citrus fruits and artificial colourings. Food allergies, especially to wheat gluten, have been linked to depression.

Nutritional deficiency is tested for using samples of blood, sweat or hair analysis. Depression has been linked to low levels of serotonin. Serotonin is made from the amino acid trypto- phan, and for the body to convert tryptophan into serotonin, vitamins B_3, B_6 and zinc are essential. Levels of these nutrients need to be kept up. A diet high in complex carbohydrates is recommended. Naturopaths suggest eating turkey, nuts, milk and bananas, as they contain tryptophan. Protein meals con- taining essential fatty acids (such as salmon and white fish) are also good choices. Vitamin C is a powerful antioxidant which can relieve stress and which many men are often deficient in. Selenium is thought to elevate mood. Low zinc levels and defi- ciencies in the B vitamins may also be linked with depression in some men.

Toxic overload is diagnosed through an analysis of symptoms and diet; fasting may be recommended to clear the system. A diet high in sugars and saturated fats leads to fatigue and depression. Alcohol, caffeine and processed foods, as well as smoking, deplete the body of essential nutrients and increase the risk of depression.

SOOTHING THERAPIES

Soothing colours can be a good antidote to depression by calm- ing the activity of over-stimulated brain waves. Colour therapists often recommend blue to promote feelings of serenity and heal- ing, and orange to keep the spirits up when they are low.

Music can uplift and inspire. Whether it's Mozart, Beethoven, Mantovani or the Verve, music can soothe a troubled mind. But music does more than uplift, inspire and soothe; regular rhythms and tonal structures can elicit suppressed feelings in need of expression and catharsis.

T'AI CHI AND YOGA

T'ai Chi is a gentle art that employs meditation and calm, smooth dance movements to improve the health of mind, body and spirit. Breathing should be co-ordinated with the movements. In order to make a significant difference to health, t'ai chi needs to be practised regularly.

Like t'ai chi, yoga pays attention to breathing and incorporates meditation. Yoga poses keep the joints and muscles flexible, build strength and promote health through nourishing the internal organs with breathing and movement. Salutary effects on the immune system have also been attributed to it. Many of the poses have masculine names – like two of the balancing poses, called the Eagle and the Warrior.

Warning: Many natural remedies, such as herbal preparations, are available at chemists and health stores, but self-medication is not usually advised and you should always consult a qualified practitioner. Make sure also that you check with a doctor that the medications are safe and do not interact with any current medication.

If you want any further information on any of these therapies, or others not listed here, you should contact the Council for Complementary and Alternative Medicine (see Resources chapter), an impartial organization which acts on behalf of consumers of natural medicine, as well as promoting research into the safety and effectiveness of alternative therapies.

It is important that you and the man you care about understand the incredible range of treatments available for depression. Depression can make a man feel that he is powerless and helpless. Obtaining knowledge about how he can fight depression is one way to regain a sense of mastery. As each step is taken to combat it, a man may be able to turn the problem around and feel closer and closer to recovery.

Encouraging a depressed man to be patient and flexible in his search for the right treatment, by being patient and flexible yourself, is crucial, as is your support throughout the treatment process. You need to have faith in his ability to get better. You need to believe that healing can happen. You need to be convinced that life is going to move forward again.

11

Moving Forward

In the depths of winter, I finally learned that within me there lay an invincible summer.

Albert Camus

When a man you care about is depressed, you probably often wish that life would get back to normal, for things to return to the way they once were. But how can things ever be exactly the same again? The experience has changed you, the man who is depressed, and your relationship.

When a man recovers from his depression, things can't go back to the way that they were, but surprisingly you may find that you don't want them to. You may have found a new way of living that is actually better. This is not to say that depression is positive. It is simply to say that the solutions and coping strategies you have developed may have helped you both grow and change.

In your role as helper, you will have struggled with feelings of anxiety, despair and helplessness. You will have questioned your ability to cope. You will have questioned your relationship. But you will also have found that you are stronger than you think. The experience of his depression may have left you shell-shocked and scarred. Yet these scars signal that you are capable of overcoming adversity, and as such they are sources of empowerment.

You will have learned that you can cope with difficulties and change, and that it is OK to make mistakes. And by exploring and understanding how another person's depression affects you, you will be better able to understand your own strengths and weaknesses. Your exploration won't be easy or painless, but to quote Plato 'The unexamined life isn't not worth living.'

And the man who has experienced depression will have come face-to-face with the loneliness, confusion and play-acting that are features of so many men's lives.

Depression is thought by some to be a message from the body that there is a need to address an imbalance in a person's life. Many men today are still struggling to overcome the legacy of poor communication skills, emotional timidity and hostile competitiveness which has been handed down to them. Depression may alert a man to the pain he has been hiding beneath an 'I'm fine' masquerade.

If a man can emerge from the experience of depression and feel more comfortable with his feelings, better able to be close to others, and with a clearer idea of how to find fulfilment in his life, then the process can be a powerful and potentially creative healing path for him.

And, as both of you change and grow, you may also find that your relationship has changed.

The mutual affection you have for each other may have grown deeper. If you have shown him that you accept him no matter how bad he is feeling; if you have learned to communicate with openness, honesty, trust and acceptance; if his emotional pain has forced him to reach out and acknowledge his feelings and you have responded with caring and support, then it is likely that the bonds between you have been strengthened.

On the other hand, you may find that he doesn't want you in his life anymore. You remind him too much of bad times. This may be painful for you, but the experience may have highlighted differences between you. If the man you care about feels uncomfortable around you because you have seen him at his most vulnerable, don't feel rejected or try to force yourself into his life. It isn't anything you have done. It is time for you to accept change.

Or you may find that he does want you in his life, but not in the way you think.

Maureen was convinced she had done something wrong when her father, who had suffered from severe depression since he'd lost the use of his arm in a car crash two years previously, told her that she didn't need to call round to see him quite so often. When she asked her father what was going on, he told her that she had done nothing wrong, she had done everything right. It was just that, even though he wasn't fully recovered yet, he felt that he could cope on his own again.

If a man tells you that he thinks he can cope again without you, you can remain watchful and let him know you are there if things become difficult, but you need to accept that your role as a helper for him could be over.

It's good news when a man doesn't need your support so much – it means that he is dealing with his problems and life can move on. If helping him has given you a sense of purpose, made you feel good about yourself or simply dominated your thoughts, you may be surprised that mingled with your relief you also feel a little scared and sad. It's essential now to be as good at knowing when to let go as you were at knowing when he needed help.

Not all men recover from depression, but many do – however impossible this may seem at the time. When a man starts to recover, you may have to accept the final lesson about helping: letting go.

Letting go may not be easy, and a part of you will always worry, 'Could this happen again? Could we cope if it happened again?' Unfortunately, if a man has had one bout of depression it's possible that his symptoms will return, but remind yourself that you have managed to cope once, and you have coped together.

You have discovered within yourself a strength to overcome great difficulties. Use the experience as a source of empowerment and deeper connection between the two of you. And if the relationship does not last, be secure in the knowledge that, whatever the result, you gave your support. You knew what to do, how to help, and you did the best that you could.

And Finally

As your relationship with the man you care about adapts to his depression, try to use some of the recommendations in this book to change the way you interact with each other and avoid the depressive dance. Throughout his depression, remember:

- Take good care of yourself so that you don't become an overlooked casualty of his disorder.
- Be as informed and as educated as you can about depression and its effects on relationships, but at the same time don't ignore your own feelings and intuitions.
- Offer him your unqualified support, but know what your limits are.
- Keep to your routine as much as possible.
- Share your feelings.
- Don't take his depression personally.
- Ask for help if you need it.
- Try to work as a team.
- You are stronger than you think.

Most important, bear in mind that his depression is difficult for you as well as him. Working with him collaboratively will not just help him and your relationship, it will help you, too. You will both feel less isolated, more strong and more hopeful. You will both realize that there is reason to be optimistic.

Depression is often spoken of in terms of darkness and winter, but once the depression lifts those who have suffered speak of light and new beginnings. You can share in that new beginning. Both you and the man you care about have faced helplessness and despair, but both of you can return from the abyss with renewed strength and hope.

Depression doesn't have to destroy his life, your life or your relationship. Recovery is possible, and you may find that, despite the difficult times you have had, your life has not just moved on, it has moved forward.

Resources

Detailed information for depressed men and their families and friends can be obtained from the specialist organizations, phone helplines and websites listed below. When applying for information by post, please enclose a SAE.

UK and Ireland

Crisis Helplines

Telephone Helplines Association
http://www.helplines.org.uk.

The Samaritans
General Office
10 The Grove
Slough SL1 1QP
+44(0)1753 532713
+44(0)8457 909090 or 0345 909090 (24-hour helpline)
+353(0)1850 609090 (Republic of Ireland)
Textphone number for the hard of hearing: +44(0)8457 909192
The Samaritans is a registered charity based in the UK and Republic of Ireland which provides confidential emotional support to any person who is suicidal or despairing. The Samaritans also aim to increase public awareness of the issues surrounding depression.

If you want to contact the
Samaritans by post or email:
Chris
The Samaritans
PO Box 90 90
Slough SL1 1UU
email: jo@samaritans.org
website: www.samaritans.org

Careline
Cardinal Heenan Centre
324–6 High Road
Ilford
Essex IG1 1QP
+44(0)208 514 5444
+44(0)208 514 1177 (counselling
on all issues)

Youth Access
(counselling for young men and
boys)
1a Taylor's Yard
67 Alderbrook Road
London SW12 8AD
+44(0)208 772 9900

Irish Association for Counselling
8 Cumberland St
Dun Laoghaire
Dublin
+ 353 (0)1 230061

Abuse

Childline
Freepost 1111
London N1 OBR
+44(0)800 1111

Rape Crisis Centre
PO Box 69
London WC1X 9NJ
+44(0)207 837 1600

Survivors
(support for men who have been
raped)
PO Box 2470
London SW9 9ZP
+44(0)207 833 3737

Victim Support
+44(0)845 303 0900

Women's Aid
(for women in violent relationships)
+44(0)345 023468

Addictions

Alcoholics Anonymous
PO Box 1
Stonebow House
Stonebow
York YO1 2NJ
+44(0)1904 644026 (for local
helpline numbers)

Al-Anon Family Groups
61 Great Dover Street
London SE1 4YF
+44(0)207 403 0888

Narcotics Anonymous
UK Service Office
PO Box 1980
London N19 3LS
+44(0)207 730 0009

National Drugs Helpline
+44(0)800 776600

Carers

Carers National Association
20–25 Glasshouse Yard
London EC1 4JS
+44(0)345 573369

Carers Association
St Mary's Community Centre
Richmond Hill
Dublin 6
+353(0)1 497 6108

Counsel and Care
(support for the elderly and their
carers)
Twyman House
16 Bonny Street
London NW1 9PG
+44(0)845 300 7585

Patients Association
(details of organizations and support groups for different illnesses
and disabilities)
+44(0)208 423 8999

Young Minds
(for parents and carers worried
about a young person's mental
health)
102–108 Clerkenwell Road
London EC1M 5SA
+44(0)345 626376

RADAR
(for those with a disability and
their carers)
Unit 12
City Forum
250 City Road
London EC1V 8AF
+44(0)207 250 3222

Debt

Citizens' Advice Bureaux
For the address of your local Citizens' Advice Bureau, check the Yellow Pages under 'Counselling and Advice', or the White Pages under 'C'.

National Debtline
Birmingham Settlement
318 Summer Lane
Birmingham B18 3RL
+44(0)121 359 8501

Family Welfare Association
501–505 Kingsland Road
London E8 4AU
+44(0)207 254 6251

Depression and Mental Illness

Your first port of call should of course be your own doctor. NHS Direct can also offer advice: +44(0)845 4647.

Depression Alliance
35 Westminster Bridge Road
London SE1 7JB
+44(0)207 207 3293
website:
www.depressionalliance.org

Manic Depressives Fellowship
8–10 High Street
Kingston-upon-Thames
Surrey KT1 1EY
+44(0)208 974 6550

Depressives Anonymous
36 Chestnut Avenue
Beverly
North Humberside HU17 9QU
+44(0)1482 887634

MIND (National Association for Mental Health)
Now over 50 years old, MIND is the leading mental health charity in the UK. It aims at working towards a better life for everyone experiencing mental distress. MIND offers support if you are worried about your own mental health and that of someone else.

MIND's headquarters are London-based, but there are regional offices and local associations – see your telephone directory.

Granta House
15–19 Broadway
London E15 4BQ
+44(0)208 519 2122
Information line: +44(0)345 660163
Within London: +44(0)208 522 1728
Outside greater London: +44(0)8457 660163
website: www.mind.org.uk

SANE
2nd Floor
199–205 Old Marylebone Road
London NW1 5QP
Tel +44(0)345 678000
website:
beta.mkn.co.uk/help/extra/charity/sane/index

Seasonal Affective Disorder Association
PO Box 989
London SW7 2PZ
+44(0)1903 814942

Eating Disorders Association
First Floor
Wensum House
103 Prince of Wales Road
Norwich
Norfolk NR1 1DW
+44(0)1603 621414

Gay Issues

London Lesbian and Gay Switchboard
PO Box 7324
London N1 9QS
+44(0)207 837 7324
website: www.llgs.org.uk/info.htm

Homelessness

Shelter
+44(0)207 253 0202
London helpline: +44(0)800 446441
You can find your local Shelter Housing Advice line listed in the Yellow Pages under 'I' for 'Information Services'.

Men's Health

Books, videos and men's magazines are all good sources of information on a healthy lifestyle. Your local library should also be a source of help. Many organizations, such as Relate, publish books available in all major book-shops. It might be wise to invest in a good all-round book on men's health. All the mainstream men's magazines – *Esquire*, *GQ* and *Men's Health*, for example – carry regular articles and advice on men's emotional and physical health and well-being.

Health Information Service
+44(0)800 665544

Men's Health Helpline
+44(0)208 995 4448

The Impotence Association
Helpline: +44(0)208 767 7791
website: www.impotence.org.uk

Medical Advisory for Men's Health Matters
+44(0)208 994 8974

Health Education Authority
(general advice on healthy living, diet and exercise)
Trevelyan House
30 Peter Street
London SW1P 2HW
+44(0)207 222 5300

British Heart Foundation
14 Fitzhardinge Street
London W1H 4DH
+44(0)207 935 0185
website: www.bhf.org.uk

AIDS Helpline
+44(0)800 56712

Cancer Link
+44(0)800 132905

Men's Issues

The Centre for Men's Development
154 Stoke Newington Church Street
London N16 0JU
+44(0)207 686 1293

Everyman
Action Against Male Cancer
+44(0)800 731 9468
website: www.icr.ac.uk/everyman

Men for Change Network
Flat 6
75 Dartmouth Park Hill
London NW5 1JD
+44(0)207 482 5953

Hawthorn House
(website dedicated to issues
concerning men):
www.hawthornhouse.com/homepage

Relationship and Family Problems

CRUSE Bereavement Care
Cruse House
126 Sheen Road
Richmond
Surrey TW9 1UR
+44(0)208 940 4818

Age Concern
Astral House
1268 London Road
London SW16 4ER
+44(0)800 731 4931
website: www.ace.org.uk

Help the Aged
+44(0)800 650 650065

Anti-bullying Campaign
185 Tower Bridge Road
London SE1 2UF
+44(0)207 378 1446

Family Crisis Line
c/o Ashwood House
Ashwood Road
Woking

Surrey GU22 7JW
+44(0)1483 722533

Exploring Parenthood
(support for parents)
4 Ivory Place
20a Treadgold Street
London W11 4BP
+44(0)207 221 6681

Parentline
Endway House
The Endway
Hadleigh
Essex SS7 2AN
+44(0)1702 559900

Relate
(National Marriage Guidance
Council)
Herbert Gray College
Little Church Street
Rugby
Warwickshire CV21 3AP
+44(0)1788 573241
website: www.relate.org.uk

Relate has a network of around 130 centres nationwide which provide couple counselling for those with problems in relationships, psychosexual therapy, and relationship and family education.

British Association for Sexual and Relationship Therapy
PO Box 13686
London SW20 9ZH

Institute of Psychosexual Medicine
11 Chandos Street
Cavendish Square
London W1M 9DE
+44(0)207 580 0631

Single Concern Group Support Group
(for lonely and socially isolated men and women)
PO Box 4
High Street
Goring-on-Thames
Oxon RG8 9DN
+44(0)1491 873195

Single Again
(support for those returning to single status)
+44(0)800 731 1180

Fathers Need Families
(support for men living apart from their children)
+44(0)207 613 5060

More-to-life
(support group for people without children)
114 Lichfield Street
Walsall WS1 1SZ
Tel +44(0)70 500 37905
website: www.moretolife.co.uk

Therapy

The British Psychological Society
St Andrew's House
48 Princess Road East
Leicester LE1 7DR
Tel +44(0)116 254 9568
website: www.bps.org.uk

British Confederation of Psychotherapists
37 Mapesbury Road
London NW2 4HJ
+44(0)208 830 5173
website: www.bcp.org.uk

Psychotherapy Register
67 Upper Berkeley Street
London W1H 7QX
+44(0)207 724 9083

UK Council for Psychotherapy
Regents College
Inner Circle
Regent's Park
London NW1 4NS
+44(0)207 436 3002

British Association of Behavioural
and Cognitive Psychotherapists
(BABCP)
PO Box 9
Accrington BB5 2GD

The British Association for
Counselling and Psychotherapy
1 Regent's Place
Rugby
Warwickshire CV21 2BJ
+44(0)870 443 5252

Council for Complementary and
Alternative Medicine
179 Gloucester Place
London NW1 6DX
+44(0)208 735 0632

The Mental Health Association of
Ireland
Mensana House
6 Adelaide Street
Dun Laoghaire
Co, Dublin
+353 (0)1 2841166

US

National Alliance for the Mentally
Ill (NAMI)
2101 Wilson Blvd
Suite 302
Arlington, VA 22201
+1(703) 524-7600
Good source of support for families of people who are mentally ill – will provide information about local support groups.

Depression Awareness, Recognition
and Treatment (DART)
National Institute of Mental Health
5600 Fishers Lane
Rockville, MD 20857
+1(800) 421-4211

National Foundation for Depressive
Illness (NAFDI)
P.O. Box 2257
New York, NY 10116
+1(800) 248-4344

National Depressive and Manic
Depressive Association (NDMDA)
730 North Franklin Street
Suite 501
Chicago, IL 60610
+1(800) 826-3632

National Mental Health Consumer's
Self-help Information Clearinghouse
211 Chestnut Street
Suite 1000
Philadelphia, PA 19107
+1(215) 751-1810
+1(800) 553-4539

Depression and Related Affective
Disorders Association (DRADA)
Meyer 4-181
600 North Wolfe Street
Baltimore, MD 21205
+1(301) 955-4647

American Association of
Suicidology
2459 South Ash
Denver, CO 80222

American Psychological Association
750 1st Street, NE
Washington, DC 20002
+1(202) 336-5500

American Psychiatric Association
1400 K Street, NW
Washington, DC 20005
+1(202) 682-6066

National Organization for Seasonal
Affective Disorder (NOSAD)
P.O. Box 40133
Washington, DC 20016

Related Areas

Administration on Aging
330 Independence Avenue, SW
Washington, DC
+1(202) 619-0724

American Anorexia/Bulimia
Association
293 Central Park West, Suite 1R
New York, NY 10024
+1(212) 501-8351

American Association of Retired
Persons (AARP)
601 E Street, NW
Washington, DC 20049
+1(800) 424-2277

AIDS Hotline
+1(800) 342-AIDS

Anxiety Disorders Association of
America
6000 Executive Boulevard
Suite 513
Rockville, MD 20852
+1(301) 231-9350

National Clearinghouse for Alcohol
and Drug Information
P.O. Box 2345
Rockville, MD 20847-2345
+1(301) 468-2600
+1(800) 729-6686

Al-Anon Family Group Headquarters
+1(212) 302-7240

Alcoholics Anonymous World Services
+1(212) 870-3400

National Council on Alcoholism and Drug Dependence
12 West 21st Street
New York, NY 10010
+1(800) NCA-CALL

Contact (crisis line)
+1(972) 233–2233

Suggested Reading

Ackerman, Robert. *Silent Sons: A Book For and About Men* (New York: Simon & Schuster, 1994)

Apple, Michael and Rowena Gaunt. *Men's Health Handbook* (Metro, 1998)

Beattie, Melody. *Codependent No More and Beyond Codependency* (MJF, 1992)

Biddulph, Steve. *Manhood: An Action Plan for Changing Men's Lives* (Hawthorn, 1998)

--. *Raising Boys: Why Boys are Different and How to Help Them Become Happy and Well-Balanced Men* (Celestial Arts, 1998)

Bloomfield, Harold and Peter McWilliams. *How to Heal Depression* (Thorsons, 1995)

Bly, Robert. *Iron John: A Book About Men* (Element Books, 1990)

Carruthers, Malcolm. *Maximizing Manhood: Beating the Male Menopause* (HarperCollins, 1996)

Carter, Rosalyn with Susan Golant. *Helping Yourself Help Others: A Book for Caregivers* (Times Books, 1996)

Clare, Anthony. *On Men: Masculinity in Crisis* (Chatto & Windus, 2000)

Cochran, Sam and Fredric Rabinowitz. *Men and Depression: Clinical and Empirical Perspectives* (Academic Press, 2000)

Conway, Jim. *Men in Midlife Crisis* (Chariot Victor, 1997)

Downing-Orr, Kristina. *What to Do if You're Burned Out and Blue* (Thorsons, 2000)

Ferber, Jane and Suzanne Levert. *A Woman Doctor's Guide to Depression: Essential and Up-to-the-minute Information on Diagnosis, Treatment and Recovery* (Hyperion, 1997)

Foster, Charles. *There's Something I Have to Tell You* (HarperCollins, 1998)

Fran, Renee. *What's Happened to Mommy?* (R.D. Eastman Publishing, 1994)

Gilbert, Paul. *Overcoming Depression: A Self-help Guide to Using Cognitive Behavioral Techniques* (Robinson, 1997)

Golant, Mitch and Susan Golant. *What to Do When Someone You Love Is Depressed: A Practical, Compassionate, and Helpful Guide* (Henry Holt, 1996)

Gold, Mark. *The Good News About Depression* (Bantam Books, 1995)

Goldberg, Kenneth. *How Men Can Live As Long as Women* (Summit, 1994)

Goleman, Daniel. *Emotional Intelligence* (Bantam Books, 1995)

Gorman, Jack. *The Essential Guide to Psychiatric Drugs* (St Martin's Press, 1990)

Gray, John. *Men Are from Mars, Women Are from Venus: A Practical Guide for Improving Communication and Getting What You Want in Relationships* (HarperCollins, 1992)

Greist, John and James Jefferson. *Depression and Its Treatment* (rev. edn; American Psychiatric Press, 1992)

Gurian, Michael. *The Wonder of Boys: What Parents, Mentors and Educators Can Do to Shape Boys into Exceptional Men* (Tarcher/Putnam, 1997)

Kindlon, Dan and Michael Thompson. *Raising Boys: Protecting the Emotional Life of Boys* (Penguin, 2000)

Kramer, Peter. *Listening to Prozac* (New York: Penguin, 1993)

Levant, Ronald and William Pollack. *A New Psychology of Men* (HarperCollins, 1995)

Milligan, Spike and Anthony Clare. *Depression and How to Survive it* (Arrow, 1994)

Moir, Anne and David Jessel. *Brainsex: The Real Difference Between Men and Women* (Arrow, 1998)

Moir, Bill and Anne Moir. *Why Men Don't Iron* (HarperCollins, 1999)

Oster, Gerald and Sarah Montgomery. *Helping Your Depressed Teenager: A Guide for Parents and Caregivers* (John Wiley and Sons, 1995)

Palmer, Stephen (ed). *Introduction to Counselling and Psychotherapy: Your Essential Guide* (Sage, 2000)

Payne, Leanne. *Crisis in Masculinity* (Good News Publishers, 1985)

Podell, Ronald and Porter Shimer. *Contagious Emotions: Staying Well When Your Loved One Is Depressed* (Pocket Books, 1992)

Pope, Harrison, Philips, Katherine and Roberto Olivardia. *The Adonis Complex* (Free Press, 2000)

Quilliam, Susan. *What to Do When You Really Want To Help But Don't Know How* (Essex: Transformation Press, 1998)

Real, Terrence. *I Don't Want to Talk About It: Overcoming the Secret Legacy of Male Depression* (Gill and Macmillan, 1997)

Rosen, Laura Epstein and Xavier Francisco Amador. *When Someone You Love Is Depressed: How to Help Your Loved One without Losing Yourself* (Simon & Schuster, 1997)

Rosenthal, Norman. *St John's Wort: Your Natural Prozac* (HarperCollins, 1998)

Rowe, Dorothy. *Depression: The Way Out of Your Prison* (Routledge, 1989)

Savil, Jonathon and Richard Smedley. *No More Mr Fat Guy: The Nutrition and Fitness Programme for Men* (Vermilion, 1998)

Seligman, Martin. *Learned Optimism: How to Change Your Mind and Your Life* (Pocket Books, 1990)

Sheehy, Gail. *New Passages: Mapping Your Life Across Time* (HarperCollins, 1996)

Sheehy, Gail. *Understanding Men's Passages: Discovering the New Map of Men's Lives* (Random House, 1998)

Skog, Susan and *Healthy Living* Magazine. *Depression: What Your Body's Trying to Tell You* (Avon, 1999)

Skynner, Robin and John Cleese. *Life and How to Survive It*
(Arrow, 1997)

Somer, Elizabeth. *Food and Mood: The Complete Guide to Eating
Well and Feeling Your Best* (Henry Holt, 1995)

Styron, William. *Darkness Visible: A Memoir of Madness* (Random
House, 1990)

Tannen, Deborah. *You Just Don't Understand: Women and Men in
Conversation* (Ballantine, 1990)

Tricket, Shirley. *Coping with Anxiety and Depression*
(Sheldon, 1999)

Weiss, Joseph. *How Psychotherapy Works: Process and Technique*
(Guildford Press, 1993)

Wertheimer, Alison. *A Special Scar: The Experience of People
Bereaved by Suicide* (Routledge, 2001)

Williams, Xandria. *Beating the Blues: A Guide to Avoiding and
Lifting Depression* (Vermilion, 1995)

Witkin, Georgia. *The Male Stress Response: How to Survive Stress
in the 90s* (New Market Press, 1994)

Wurtzel, Elizabeth. *Prozac Nation: Young and Depressed in America*
(Riverhead Books, 1995)

Zuess, Jonathon. *The Wisdom of Depression: A Guide to
Understanding and Curing Depression Using Natural Medicine*
(Three Rivers Press, 1998)

Helpful Worldwide Websites

www.mentalhealth.com
Worldwide mental health home page
www.mentalhealth.com/bookah/p44-dp.html
Depression is a treatable illness: a patient's guide
www.managingstress.com
Information about different kinds of therapies and useful contacts
counsellinginfo.bizland.com

How to Get in Touch with the Authors

If after reading this book you feel you are helping more successfully or there are issues you'd like to discuss further, do write to us at the addresses below.

Theresa Francis-Cheung and Robin Grey
c/o Thorsons
HarperCollins*Publishers*
77–85 Fulham Palace Road
Hammersmith
London W6 8JB
email: TCheung7/10@aol.com;
RGrey23168@aol.com

Index